A First Look at Animals With Backbones
and
A First Look at Animals Without Backbones

by MILLICENT E. SELSAM and JOYCE HUNT

Illustrated by HARRIETT SPRINGER

AN AUTHORS GUILD BACKINPRINT.COM EDITION

AN AUTHORS GUILD BACKINPRINT.COM EDITION
Published by iUniverse, Inc.

For information address:
iUniverse
2021 Pine Lake Road, Suite 100
Lincoln, NE 68512
www.iuniverse.com

Originally published by Walker & Co.

ISBN: 0-595-29122-8

Printed in the United States of America

A *FIRST LOOK AT* SERIES

Each of the nature books for this series is planned to develop the child's powers of observation and give him or her a rudimentary grasp of scientific classification.

For Lyla Angelika Hunt

A First Look at
Animals With Backbones

There are lots of animals in the world.
Some have backbones.
Some do not.

A backbone is a row of bones under the skin
along the middle of the back.
Other bones are attached to it and make up the skeleton.

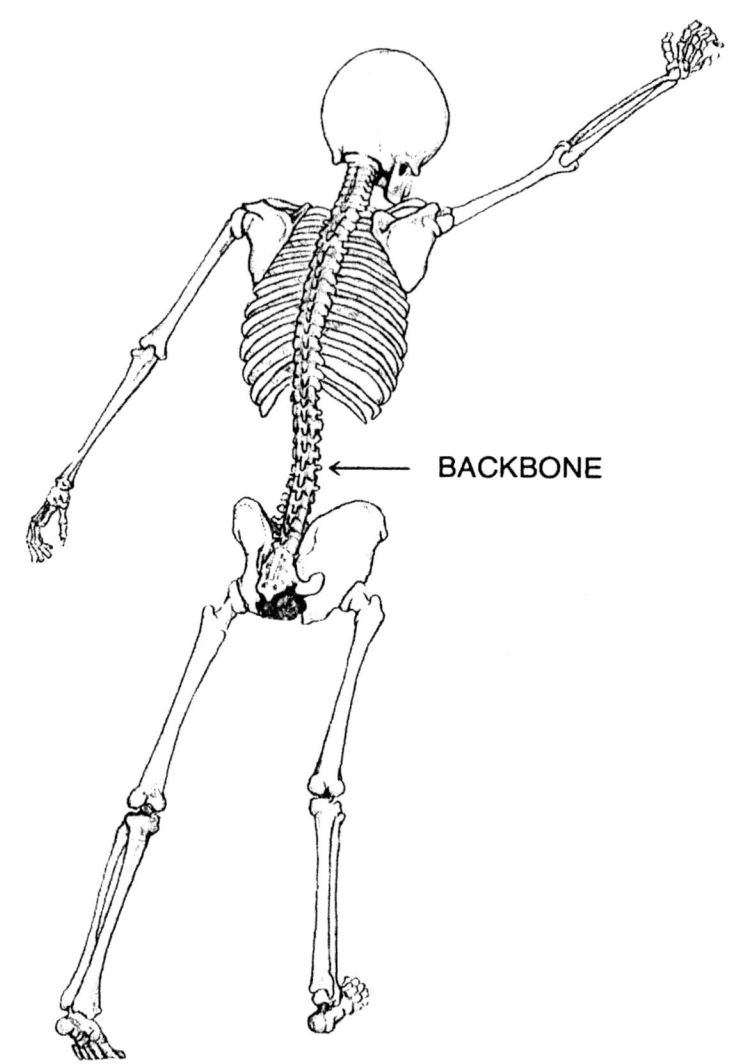

BACKBONE

This is what your skeleton looks like.

You can feel your own backbone.
Bend down and then reach behind you
to feel the bones in the middle of your back.

Any animal that has a backbone is called a vertebrate (VER-ti-brate).

Are you a vertebrate?

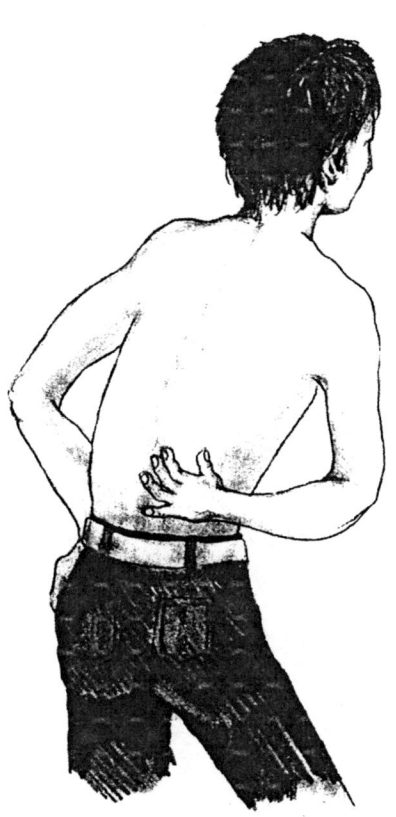

Do any of these animals have a backbone?

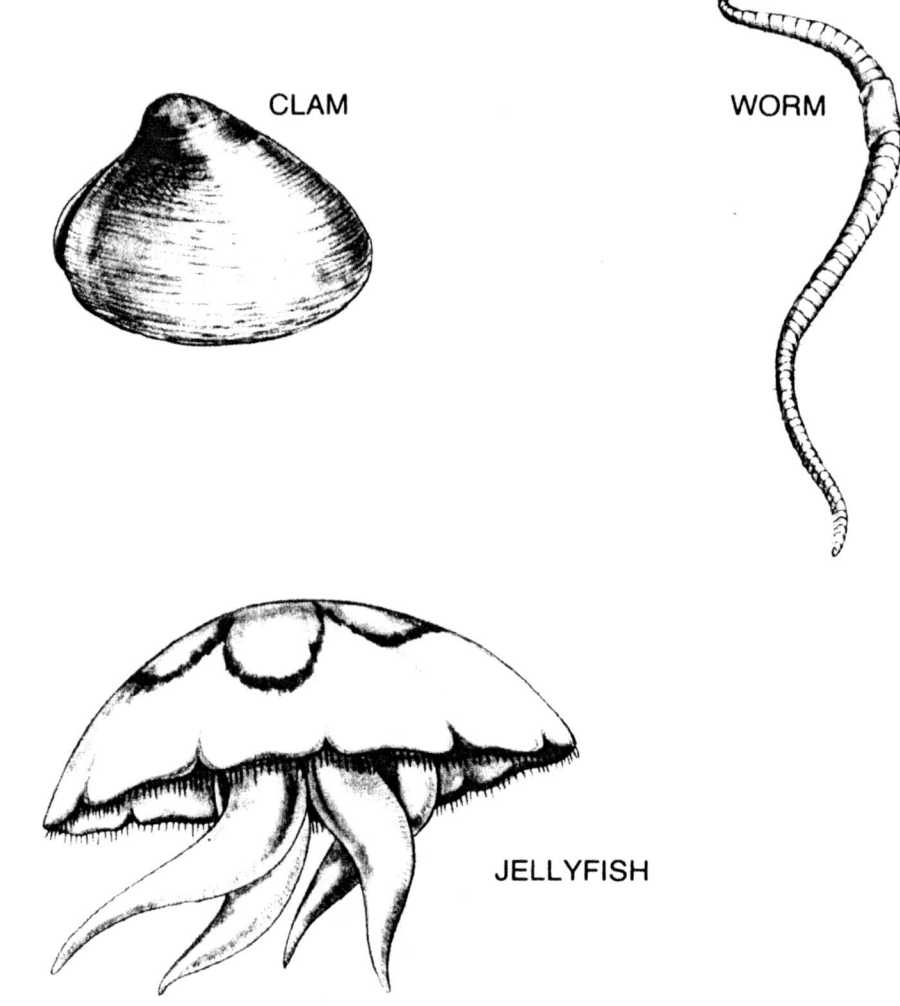

CLAM

WORM

JELLYFISH

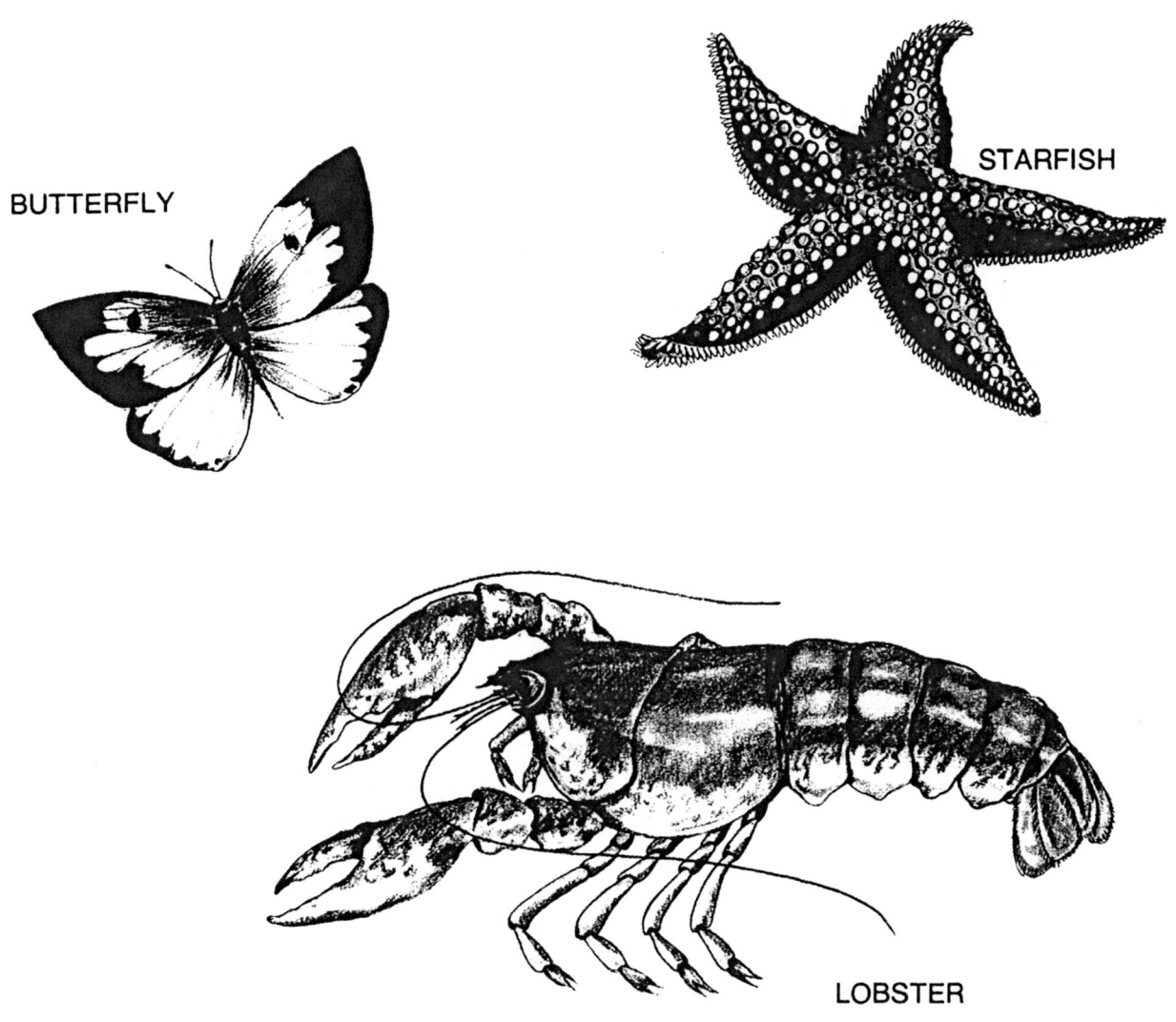

BUTTERFLY

STARFISH

LOBSTER

Although some of these animals have a hard outside covering, none of them have backbones.

They are called *in*vertebrates.

Now look at these animals.
They all have backbones.
They are all vertebrates.

FISH

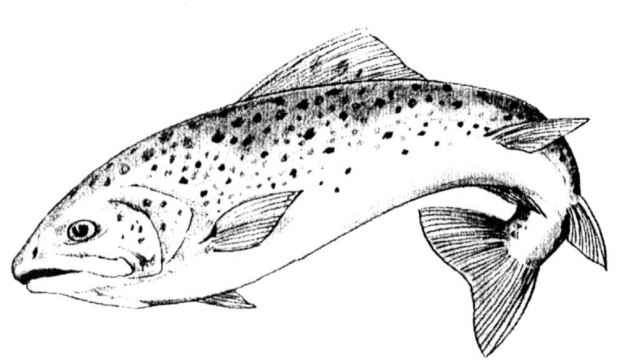

AMPHIBIANS (am-FIB-ee-ans)

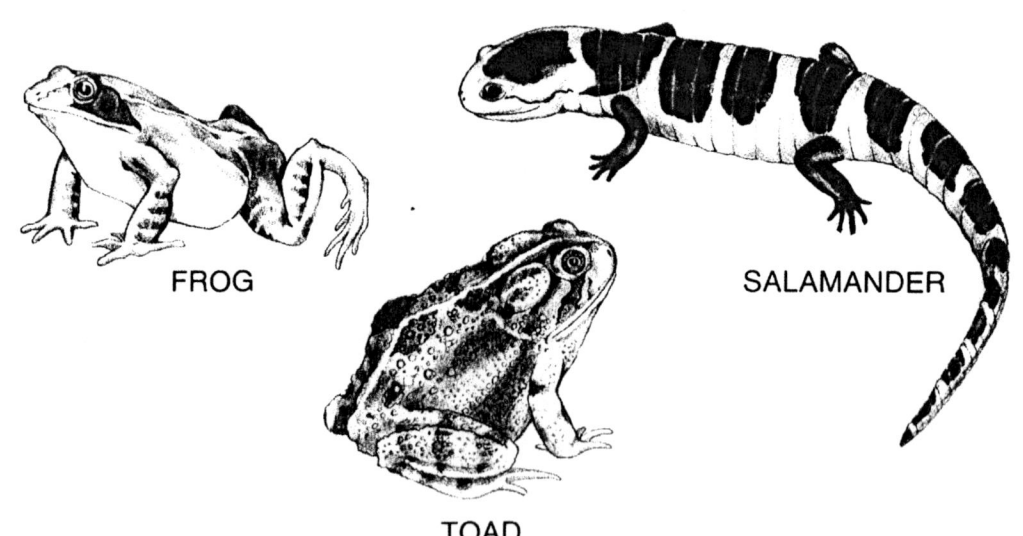

FROG

TOAD

SALAMANDER

REPTILES

SNAKE

TURTLE

LIZARD

BIRDS

MAMMALS

13

FISH

What makes a fish a fish?

A fish has a backbone.

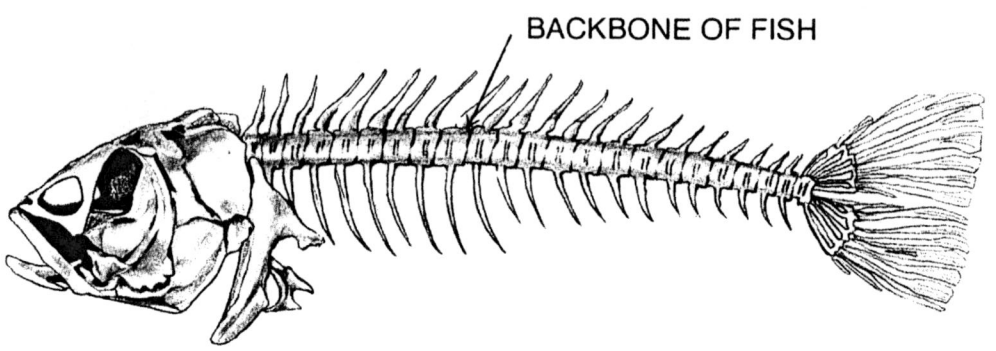

BACKBONE OF FISH

A fish breathes through gills and lives in water.

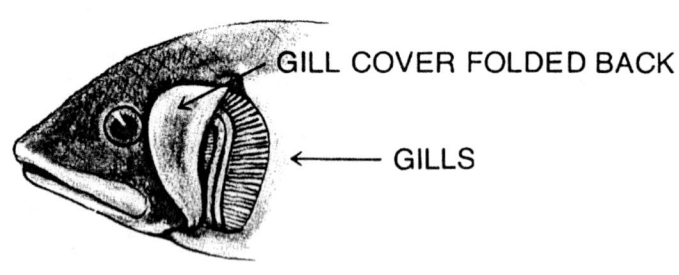

GILL COVER FOLDED BACK

GILLS

A fish has scales.

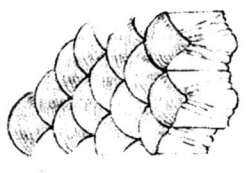

SCALES

The blood of a fish is always the same temperature
as the water it lives in.

TEMPERATURE OF WATER = 60°F

TEMPERATURE OF FISH = 60°F

And a fish has something no other animal has.
It has fins.

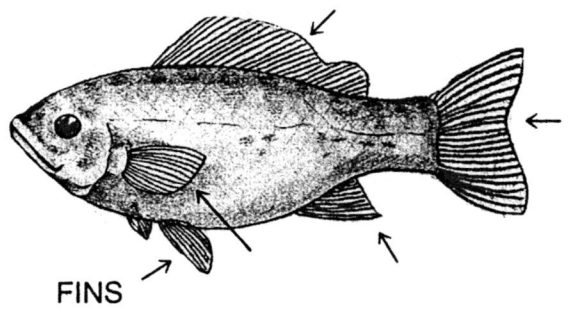

FINS

There are two big groups of fish.
Sharks and rays are in one group.
They have no real bones.
Their skeletons are made of cartilage (KAR-ti-lej),
which is softer than bone.

RAY

SHARK

It is easy to tell a shark from a ray.

The other group of fish has bones.
Most fish belong in this group.
You can tell these fish apart by looking
at the shape and the fins.

Which fish looks like a blimp?
Which fish has top fins that look like a comb?
Which fish looks like a snake?
Which fish has a tail fin like a V?

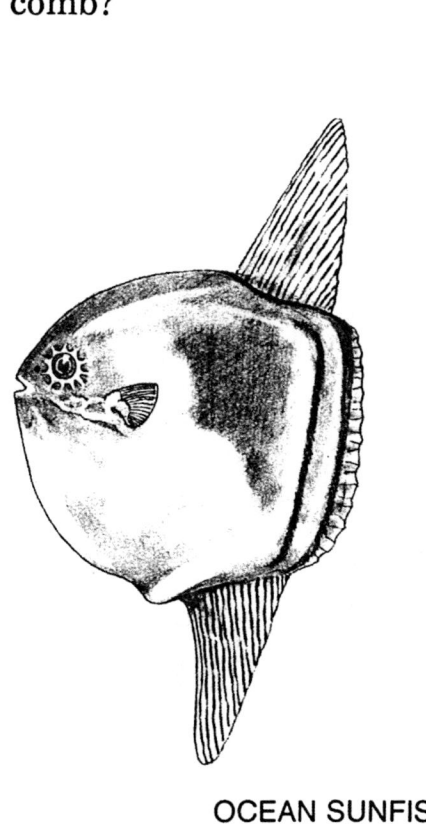

EEL

MACKEREL

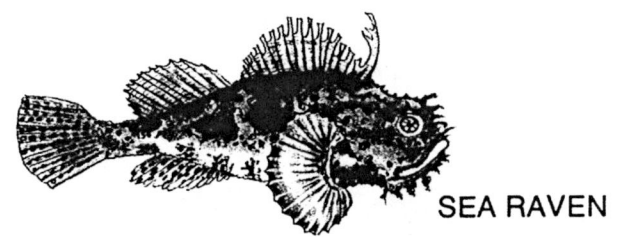

SEA RAVEN

OCEAN SUNFISH

AMPHIBIANS (am-FIB-ee-ans)

Frogs, toads, and salamanders are amphibians.

Amphibians have backbones.

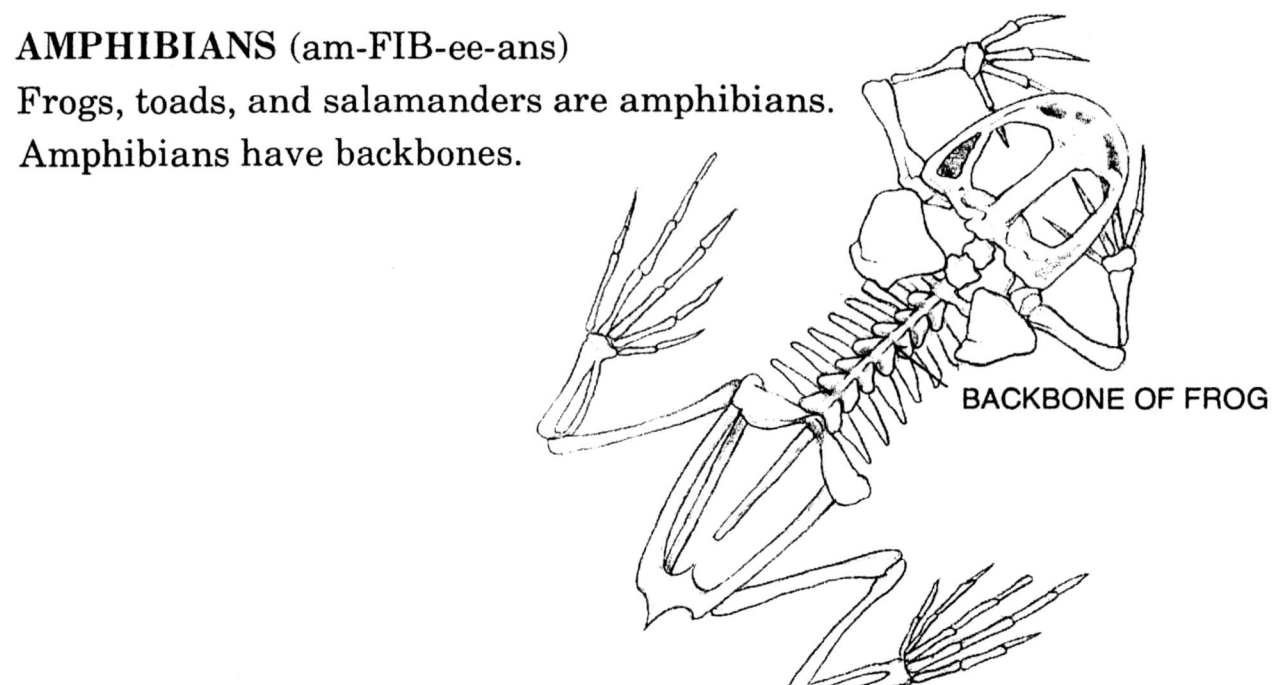

BACKBONE OF FROG

They lay their eggs in water
and spend the early part of their lives there.

A young amphibian is called a *tadpole*.
At first it has gills, but by the time it leaves the water,
it has lungs and can breathe the air on land.

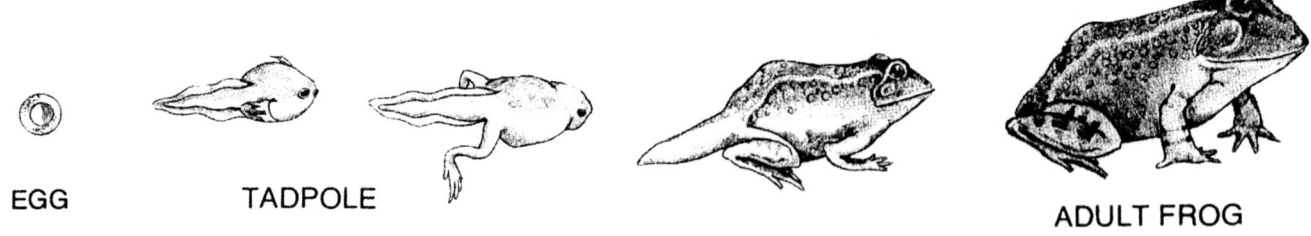

EGG   TADPOLE   ADULT FROG

Salamanders are amphibians with tails.

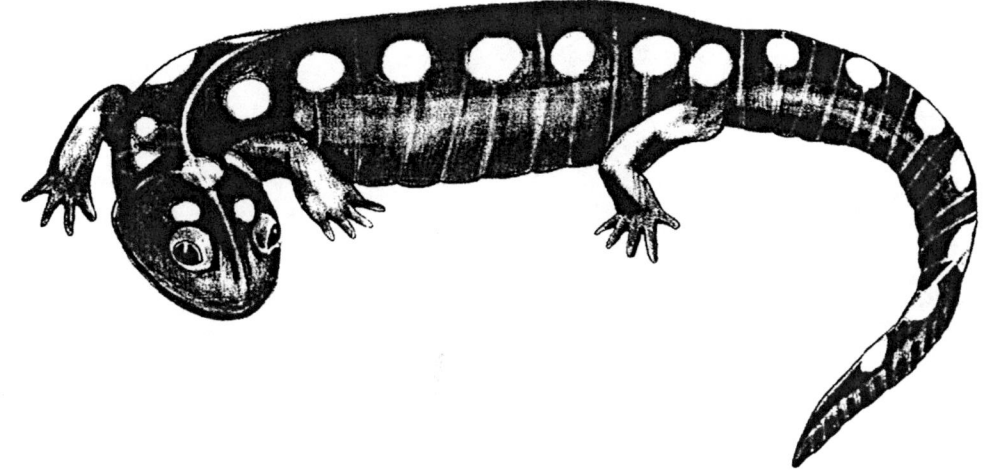

Frogs and toads are amphibians without tails.

Do you know how to tell a frog from a toad?
Look at the pictures.

TOAD   **FROG**

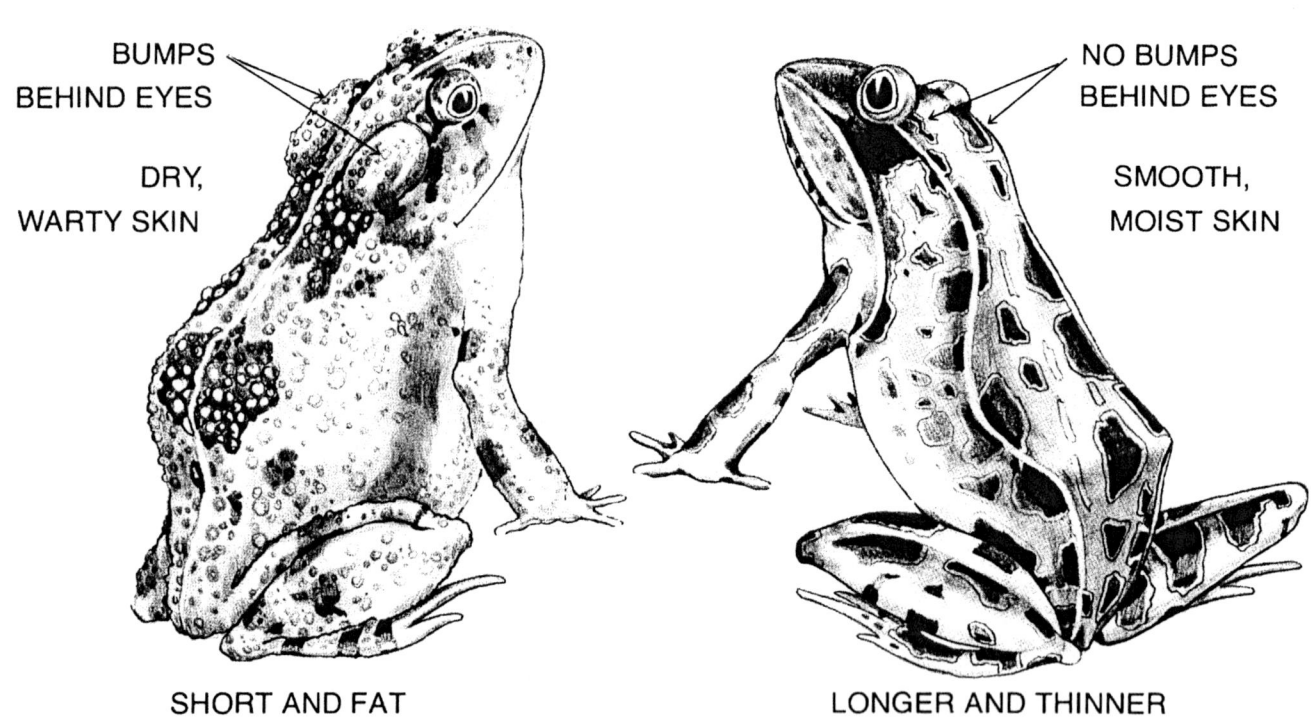

BUMPS
BEHIND EYES

DRY,
WARTY SKIN

NO BUMPS
BEHIND EYES

SMOOTH,
MOIST SKIN

SHORT AND FAT   LONGER AND THINNER

Toads lay eggs in long strings.
Frogs lay eggs in clumps.

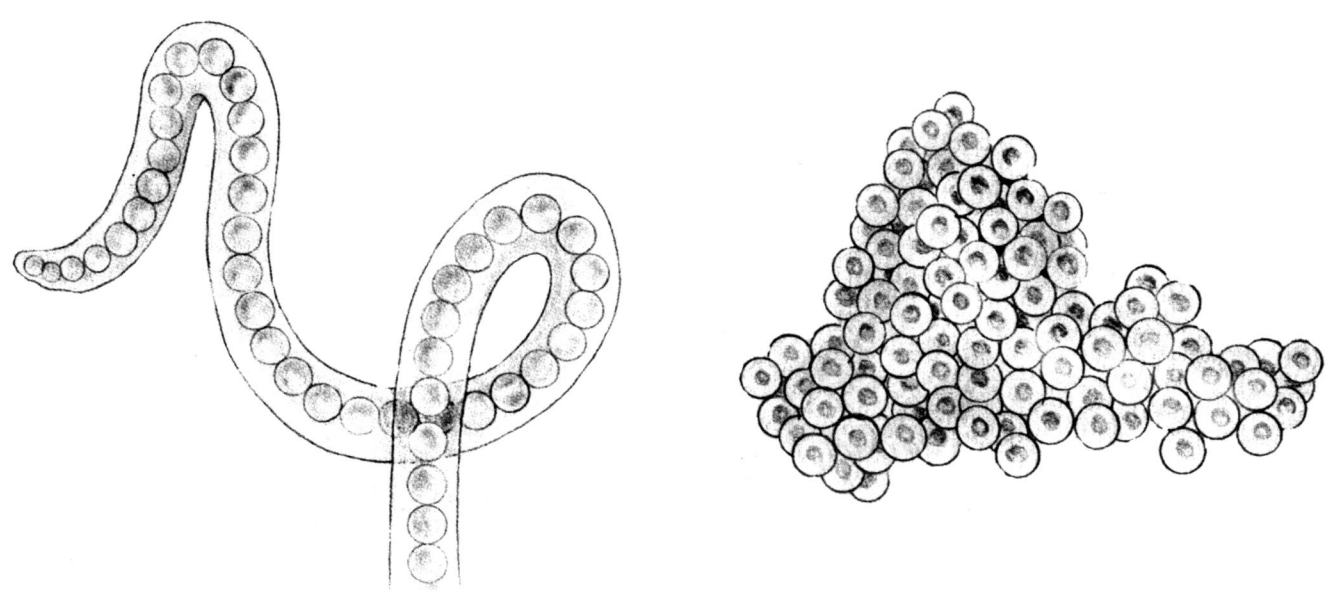

REPTILES

Snakes, lizards, turtles, and alligators are reptiles.
Reptiles have backbones.

BACKBONE OF SNAKE

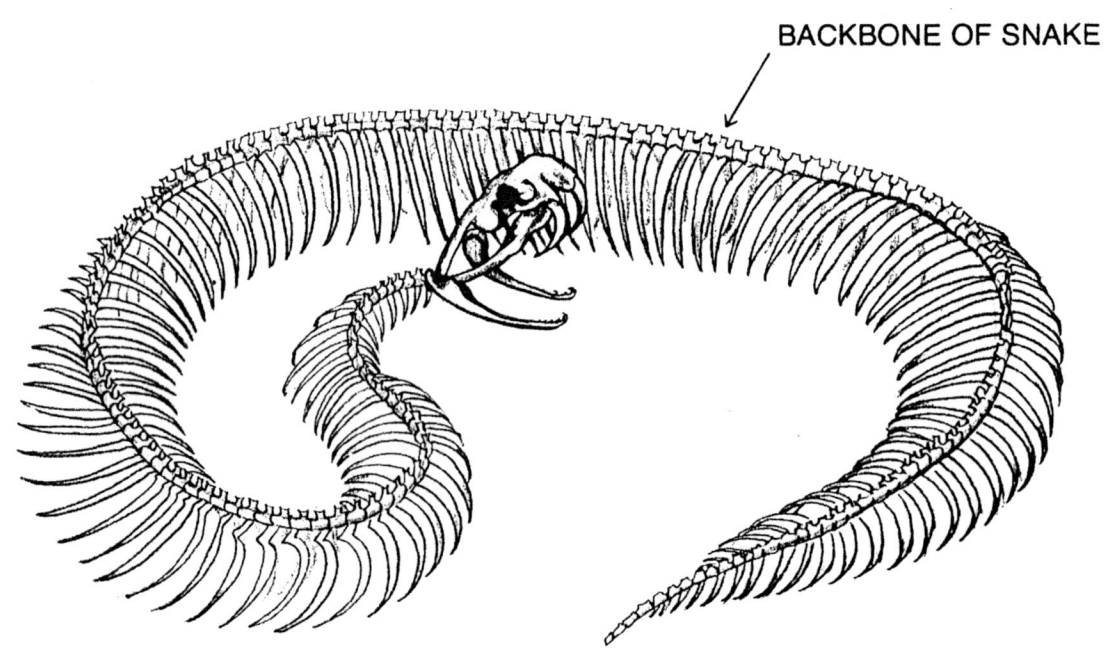

Like the fish, reptiles have scaly skins,
but these scales are tougher and harder.

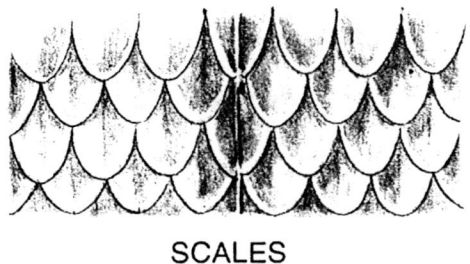

SCALES

Also reptiles do not have fins or gills.

The blood of reptiles is always the
same temperature as the air around it.

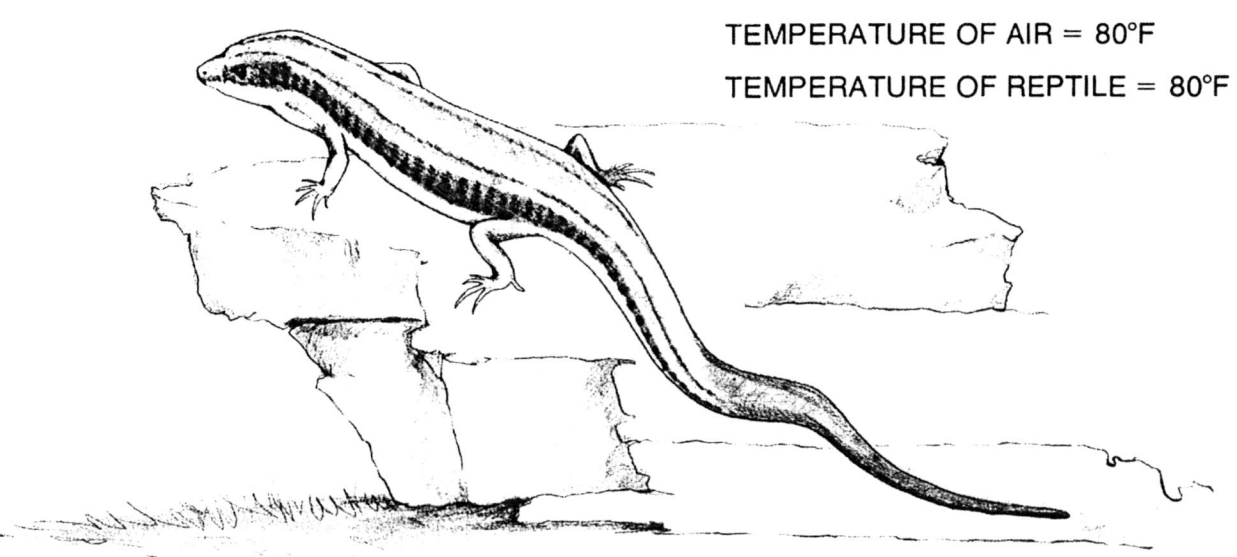

TEMPERATURE OF AIR = 80°F

TEMPERATURE OF REPTILE = 80°F

It is easy to tell reptiles apart.
Snakes have no legs.

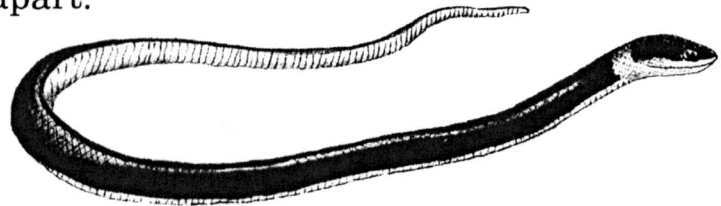

Lizards look like snakes with legs.

Lizards have eyelids and ear openings.
Snakes do not.
Here are the heads of a snake and a lizard.
Which is which?

 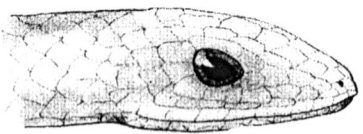

Alligators look like giant lizards.

Turtles are the only reptiles with shells.

BIRDS

What makes a bird a bird?
A bird has a backbone.

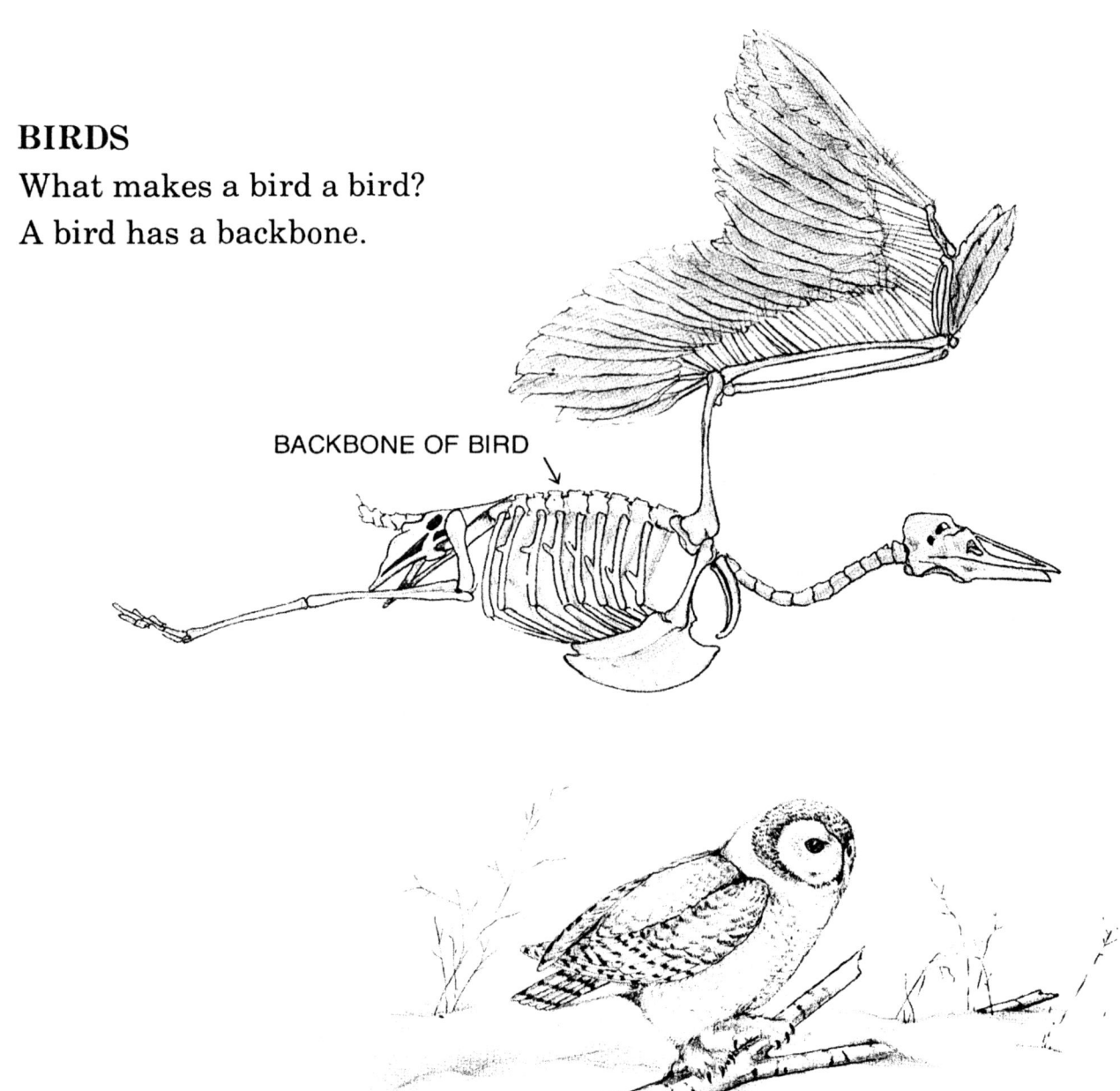

BACKBONE OF BIRD

A bird is warm-blooded.
Its blood stays warm even though
the temperature around it changes.

TEMPERATURE OF AIR = 40°F
TEMPERATURE OF BIRD = 102°F

A bird usually flies.

And a bird has something no other animal has.
It has feathers.

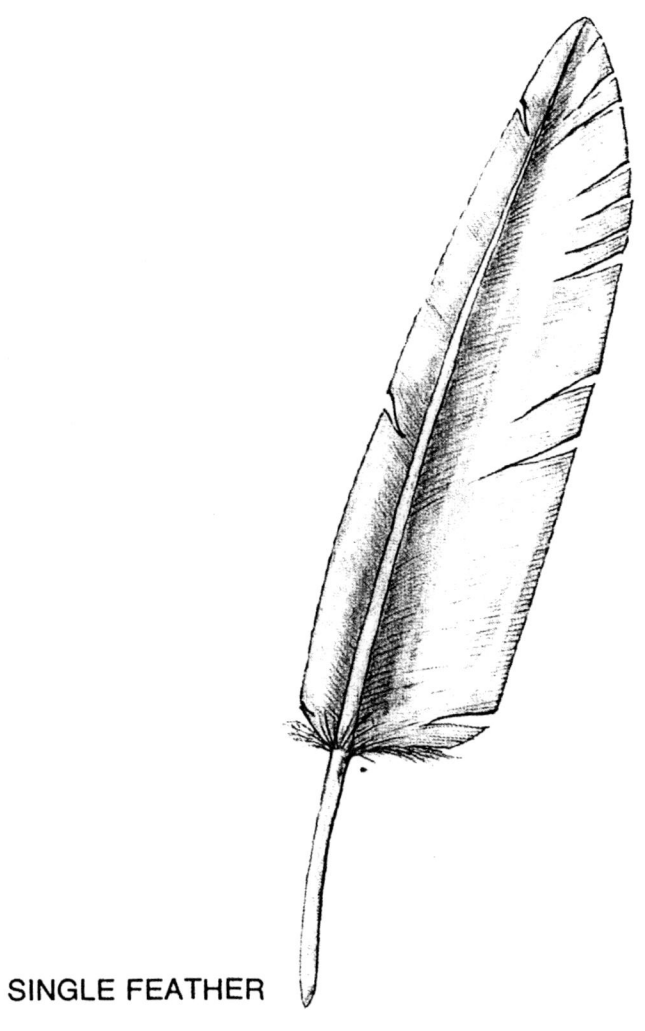

SINGLE FEATHER

Birds can be told apart by their feet.

Birds that perch have three toes in front
and one long toe behind.
Find the perching toes.

Birds that walk have three long toes in front
and one short toe behind.
Find the walking toes.

Birds that swim have webbed feet.
Find the swimming toes.

Birds that climb have two toes in front
and two toes behind.
Find the climbing toes.

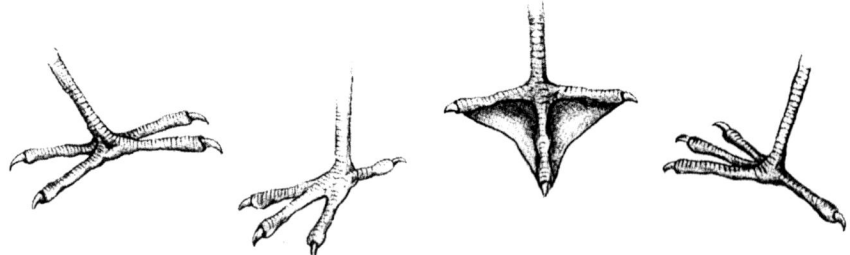

Birds are also told apart by their bills.

Birds with short, pointed bills usually eat insects.
Find the insect-eating bill.

Birds with short, thick, cone-shaped bills
usually crack seeds.
Find the seed-cracking bill.

Birds with hooked bills usually tear the flesh of small animals.
Find the flesh-tearing bill.

Birds with long, pointed bills usually catch fish.
Find the fish-eating bill.

MAMMALS

Animals with hair or fur are called mammals.

Mammals have backbones.

They are warm-blooded animals.

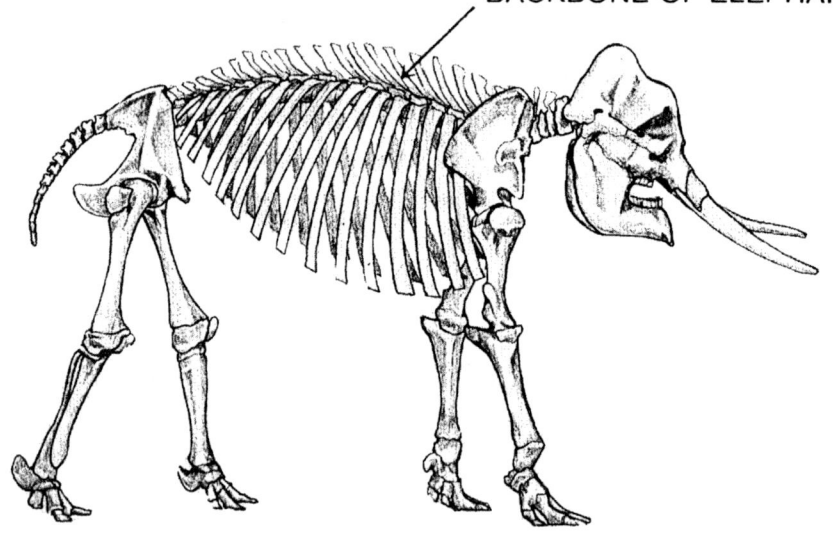

BACKBONE OF ELEPHANT

They also feed their babies milk from special parts
of their bodies called *mammary glands*.

Mammals are put in the same group
if they have the same kind of teeth.

Mammals that have sharp eyeteeth tear flesh.
Which are the flesh-tearing teeth?

Mammals that have two large front teeth on
top and bottom gnaw wood, nuts, and seeds.
Which are the gnawing teeth?

BEAVER

LION

Mammals are also told apart by their feet.

Some have three toes.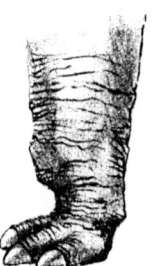
RHINOCEROS

Some have two toes.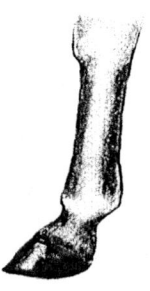
PIG

Some have one toe.
HORSE

Some have no feet
but have flippers instead.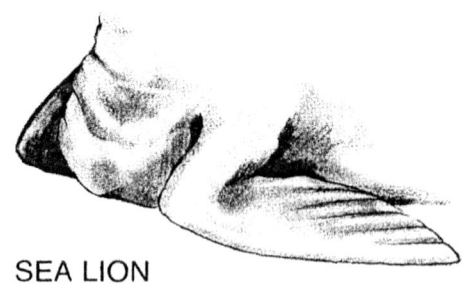

SEA LION

Some mammals have special parts that
no other mammal has.

An elephant has a trunk.

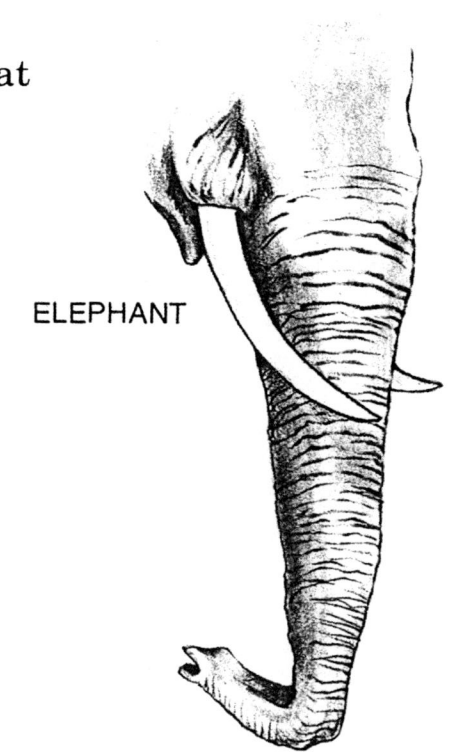

ELEPHANT

A bat has wings.

BAT

Mammals with large brains and hands that can grasp things
are in a special group.

MONKEY

HOW TO TELL THE VERTEBRATES APART:

Fish have fins.

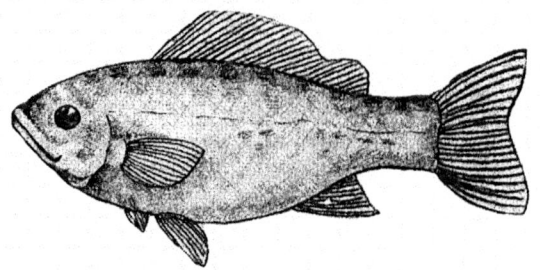

Amphibians lay their eggs in water
and spend the early part of their lives there.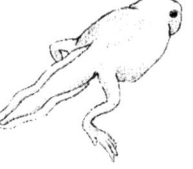

Reptiles have scaly skins
but no gills or fins.

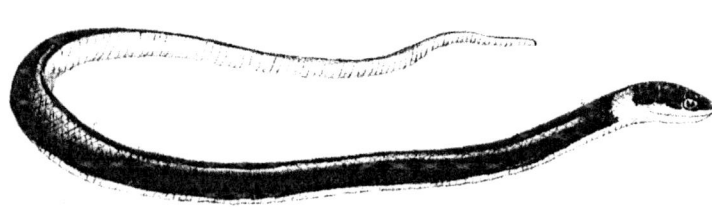

Birds have feathers.

Mammals have hair and feed their babies milk.

A First Look at
Animals Without Backbones

BACKBONE

Any living thing that is not a plant
is an animal.
Most animals that we know
have backbones.
A backbone is a row of bones along
the middle of the back.
Other bones are attached
to the backbone.
Together they make up a skeleton.

Here is a fish.

This is what is left on your plate after you
eat a fish.

Find the backbone.

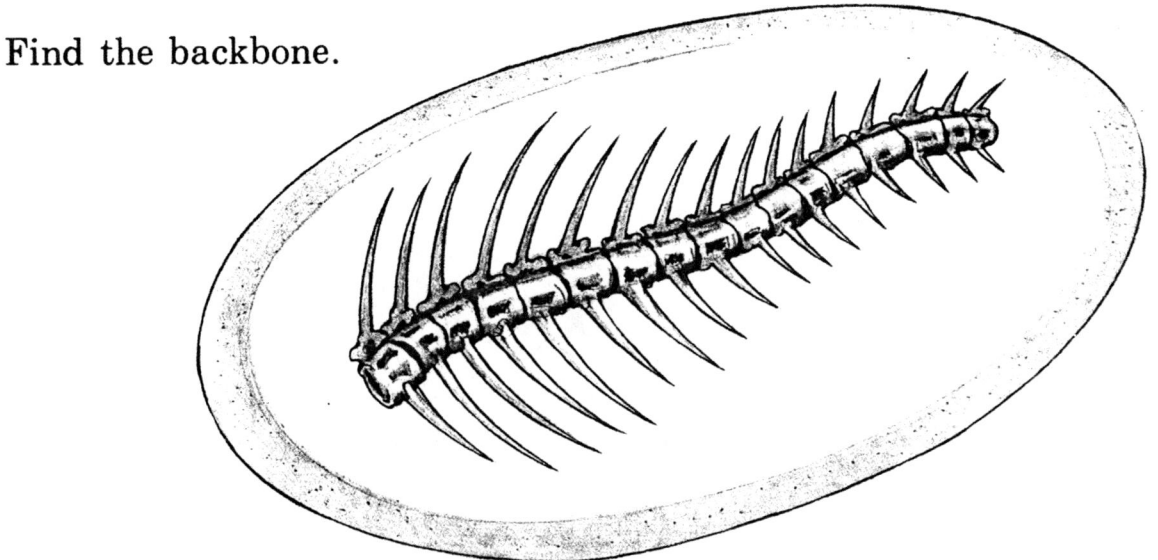

Here is a chicken.

This is what is left after you eat a chicken.
Find the backbone.

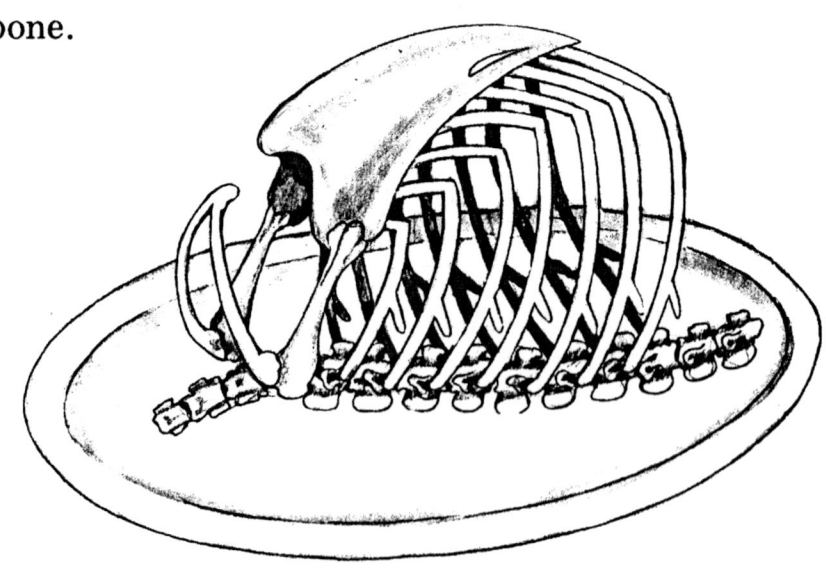

This is a snake's skeleton.
Find the backbone.

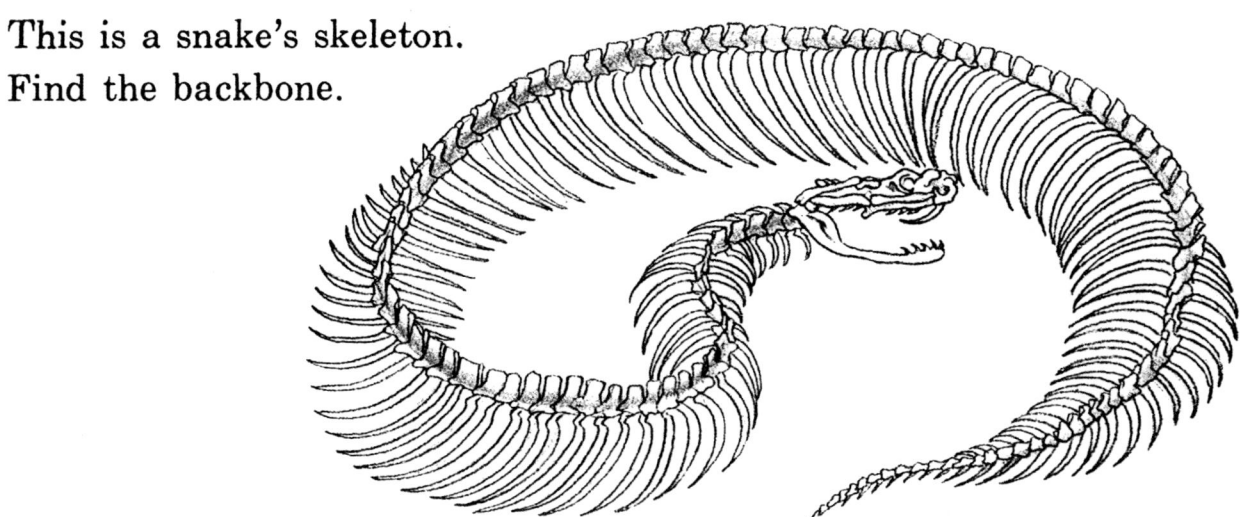

Look at the inside of this turtle's shell.

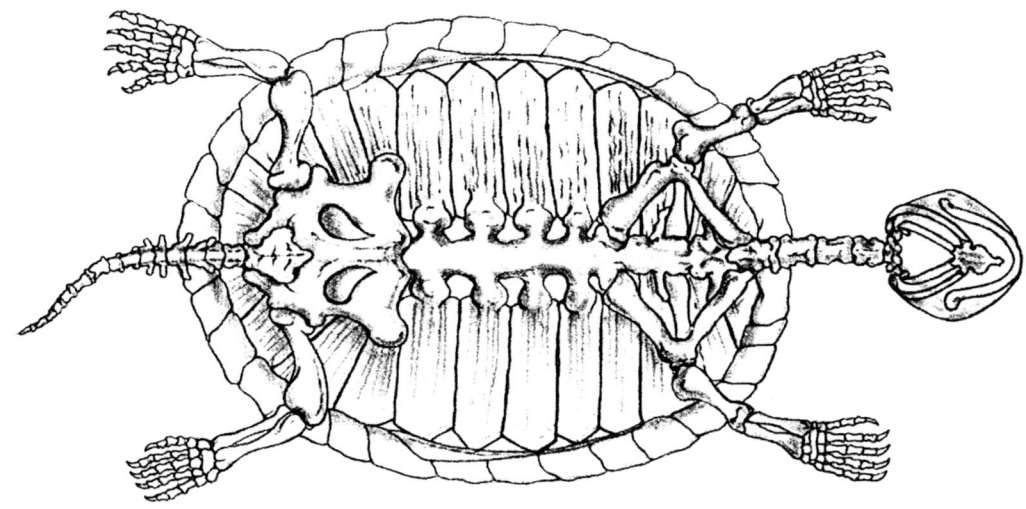

Can you see where the backbone has become
part of the shell?

Fish have backbones.

Amphibians (frogs, toads, and salamanders) have backbones.

Reptiles (snakes, lizards, turtles, and alligators) have backbones.

Birds have backbones.

Mammals (animals with hair or fur) have backbones.

All animals with backbones are called *vertebrates*.

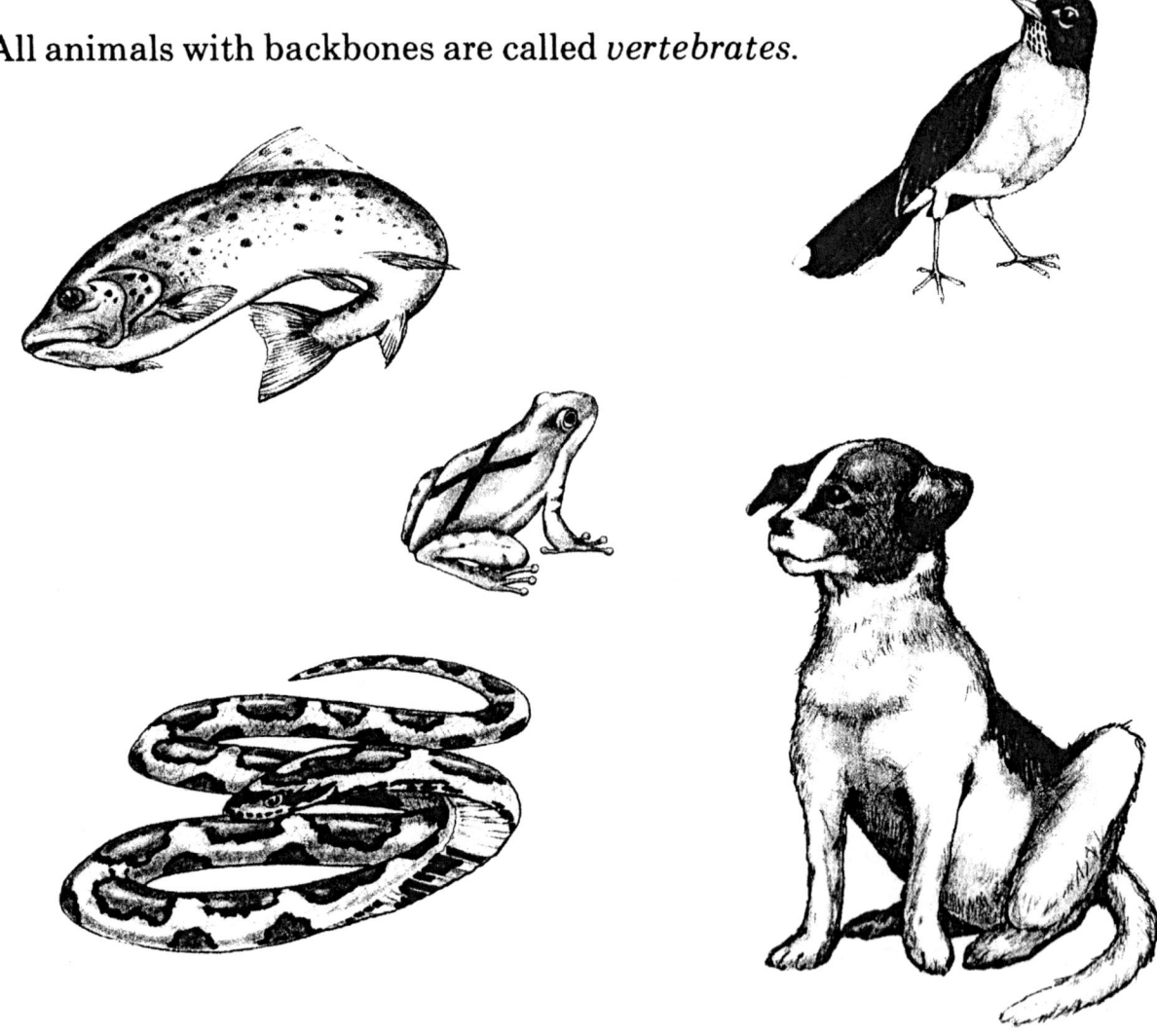

Although most of the animals we are familiar with have backbones, 95% of all animals do not have a backbone.

They are called *invertebrates* (in-VER-ta-brates).

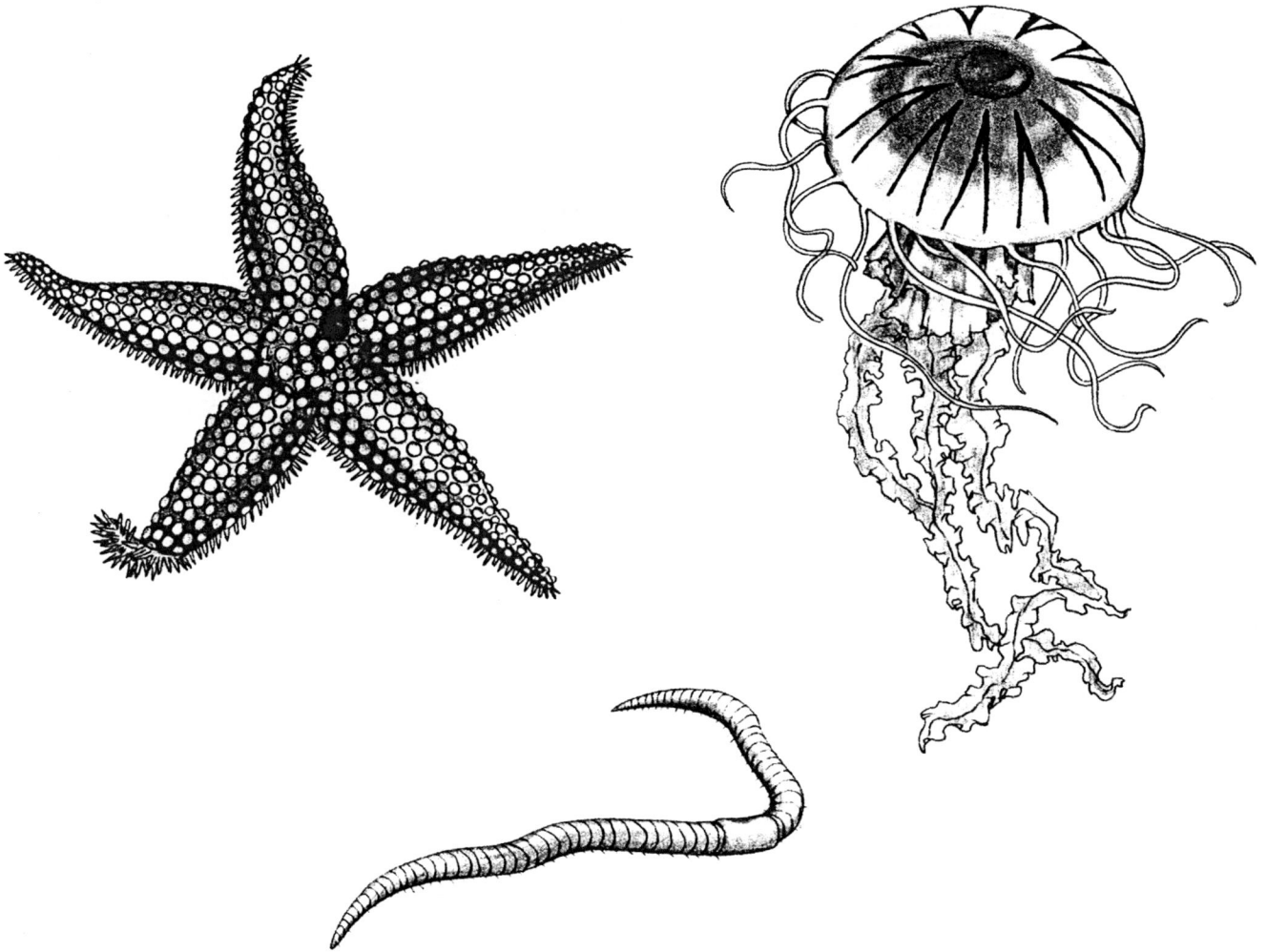

Some invertebrates have a hard covering on the outside of their bodies. This "outside skeleton" gives the body shape and protects the soft inside.

ARTHROPODS (AR-thro-pods)

Here are five animals with an outside skeleton.
They are in a group called *arthropods*.

They are different from all other invertebrates
because they have jointed legs.

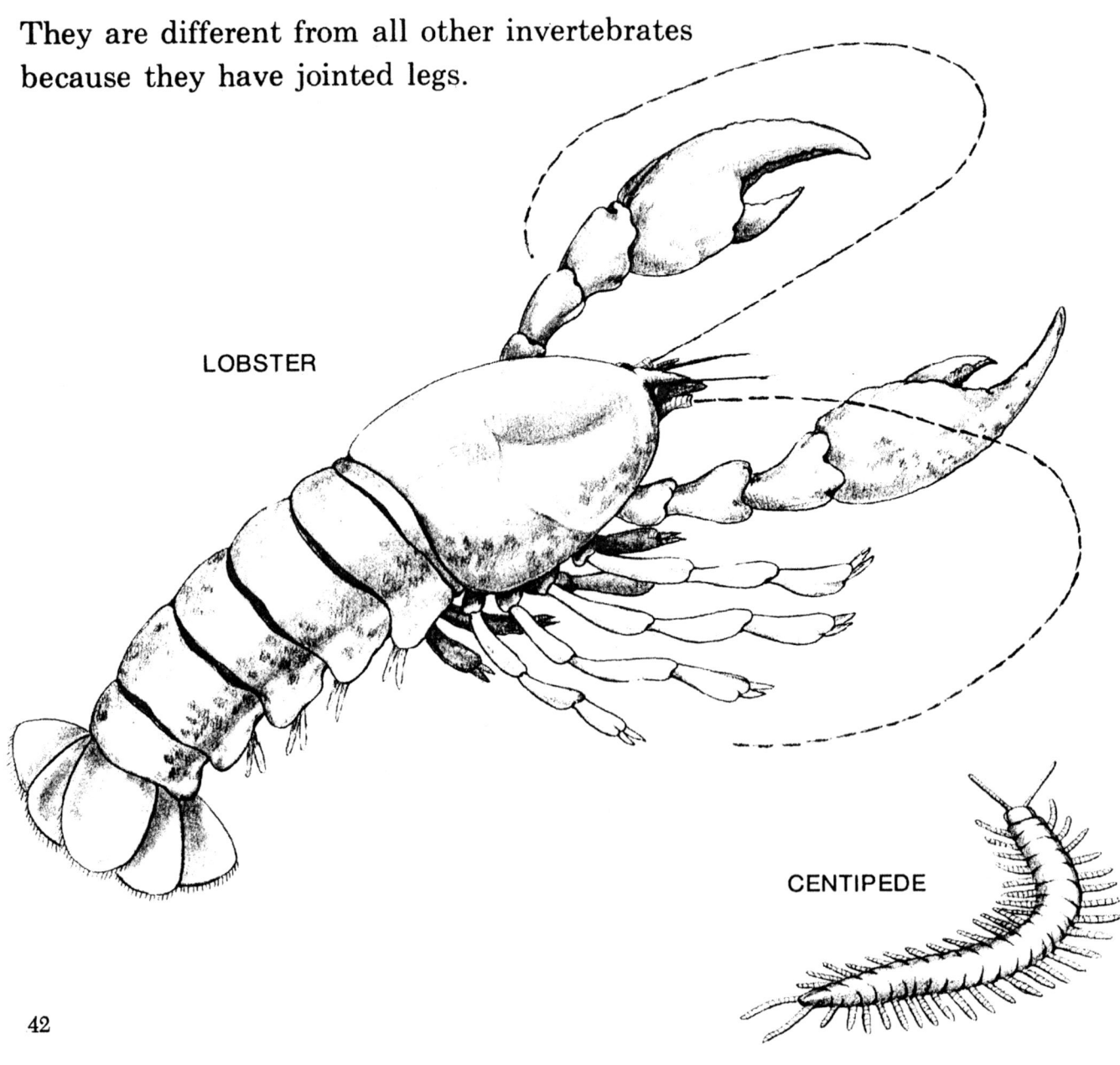

LOBSTER

CENTIPEDE

SPIDER

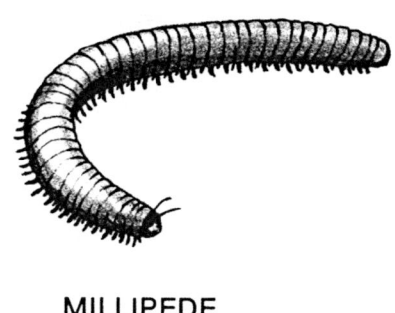

MILLIPEDE

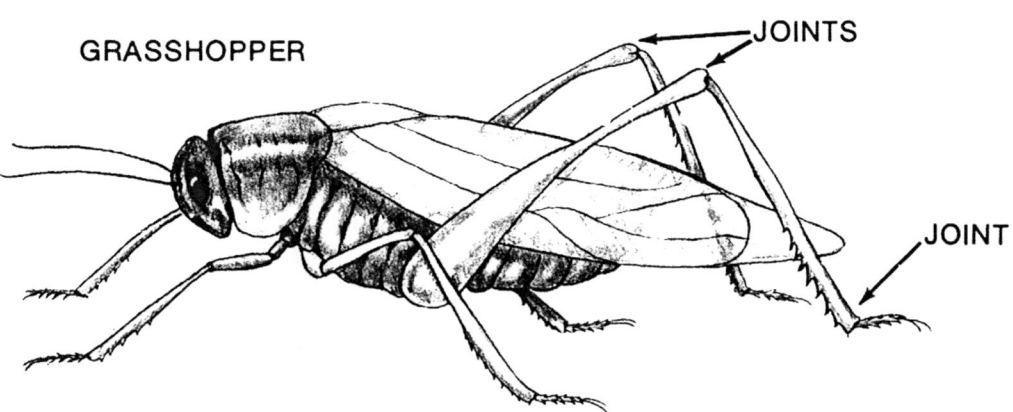

GRASSHOPPER

JOINTS

JOINT

The joints make it possible for the animal
to walk, swim, or jump.
Look for the joints in the legs.

43

All arthropods with six legs are called *insects*.

BUTTERFLY

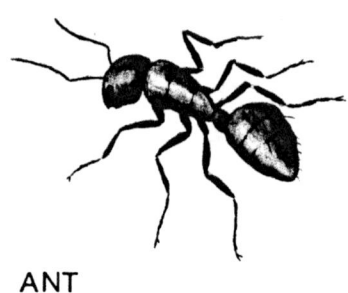

ANT

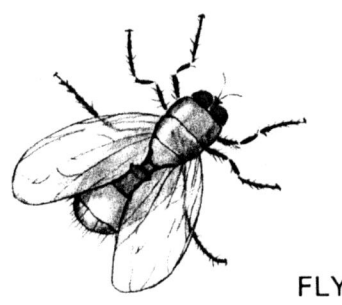

FLY

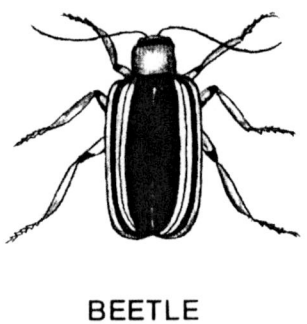

BEETLE

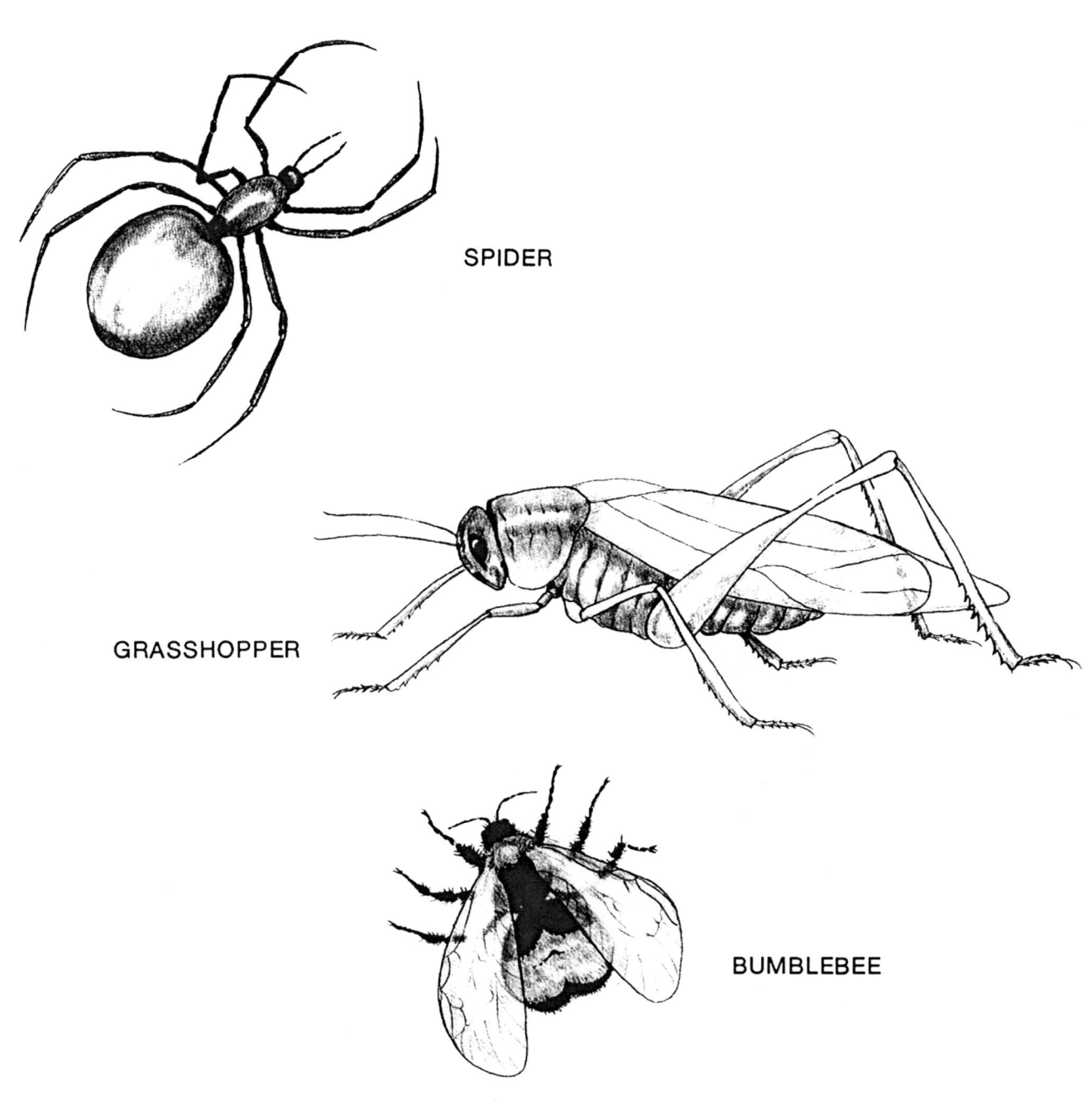

SPIDER

GRASSHOPPER

BUMBLEBEE

One of these animals does not have six legs.
Did you find it?
How many legs does the spider have?

The spider is not an insect because it has eight legs.

Are these insects?
Count the legs.

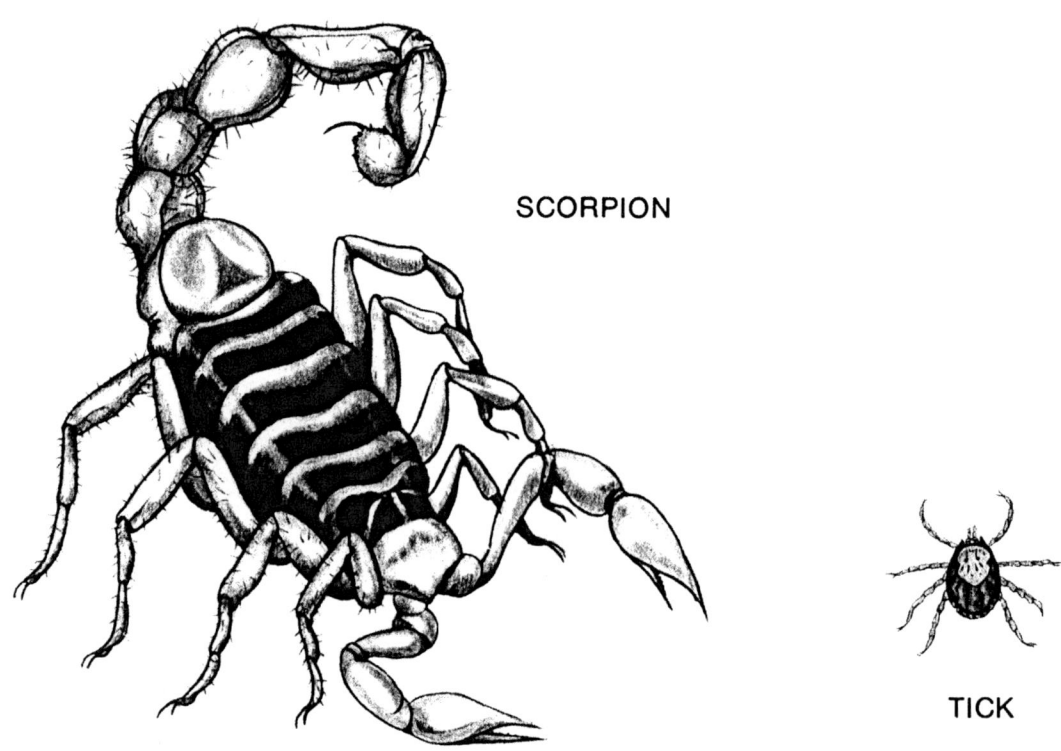

SCORPION

TICK

All arthropods with eight legs are called *arachnids* (a-RAK-nids).

Here are two animals with many legs.
Centipedes (SEN-ti-peeds) have fewer legs
than millipedes (MIL-li-peeds).
Which is which?

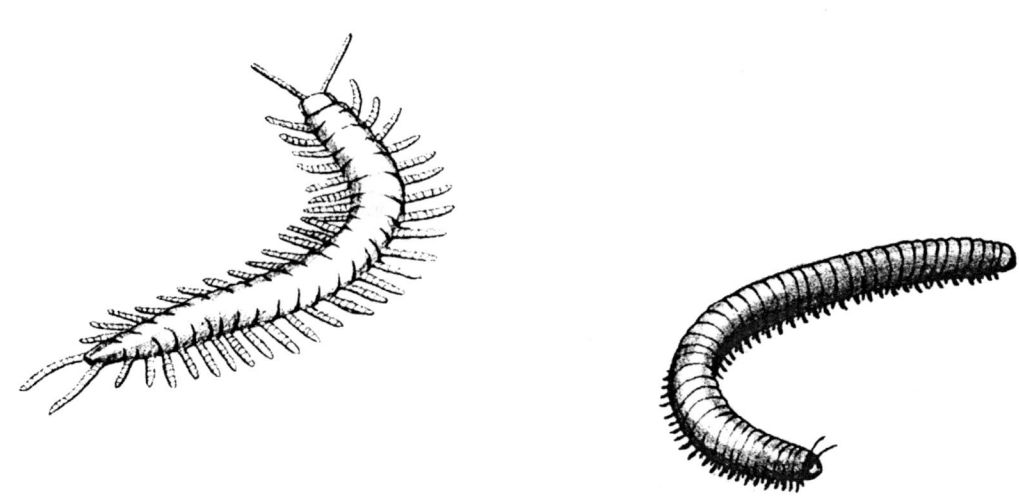

Arthropods with many jointed legs are either
centipedes or millipedes.

These invertebrates are also arthropods.
But you cannot tell them by counting their legs.
Count their antennae (an-TEN-ee) or feelers.
All arthropods with two pair of antennae are
called *crustaceans* (krus-TAY-shuns).

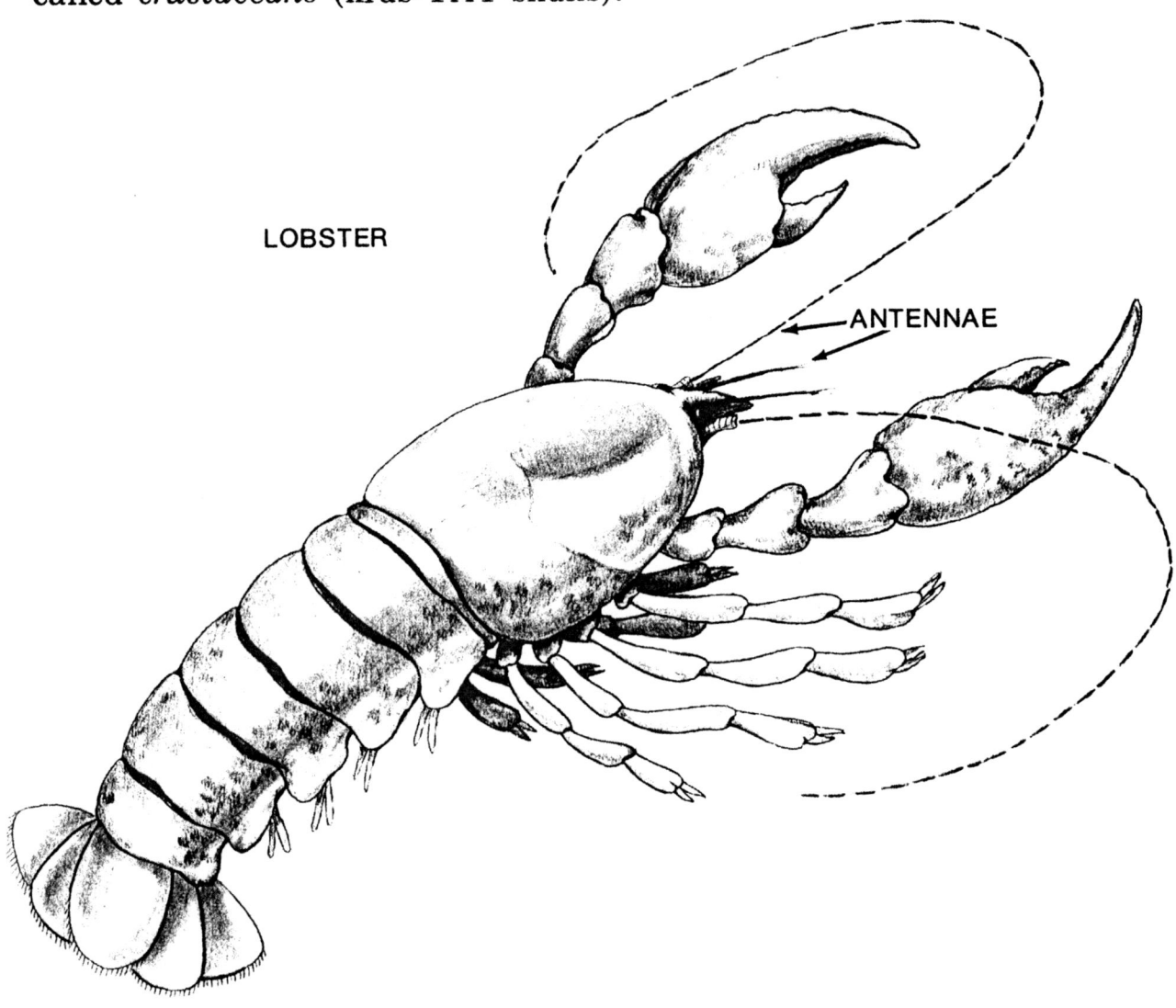

LOBSTER

ANTENNAE

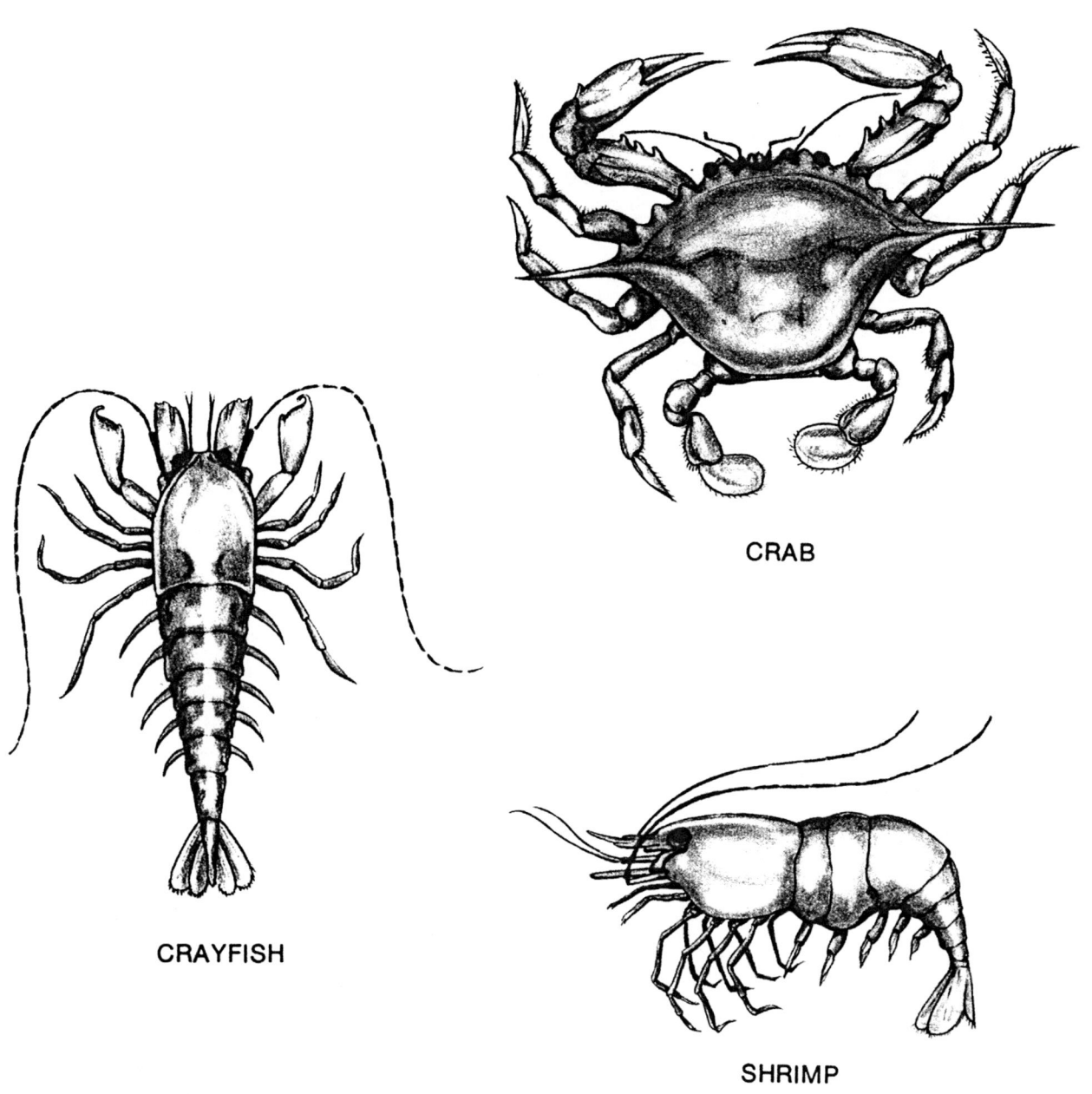

CRAB

CRAYFISH

SHRIMP

ECHINODERMS (e-KINE-o-derms)

Here are other invertebrates with a hard
covering. This time it is a spiny skin.
They are not arthropods because they do not
have jointed legs. Invertebrates with a spiny
skin are called *echinoderms*.

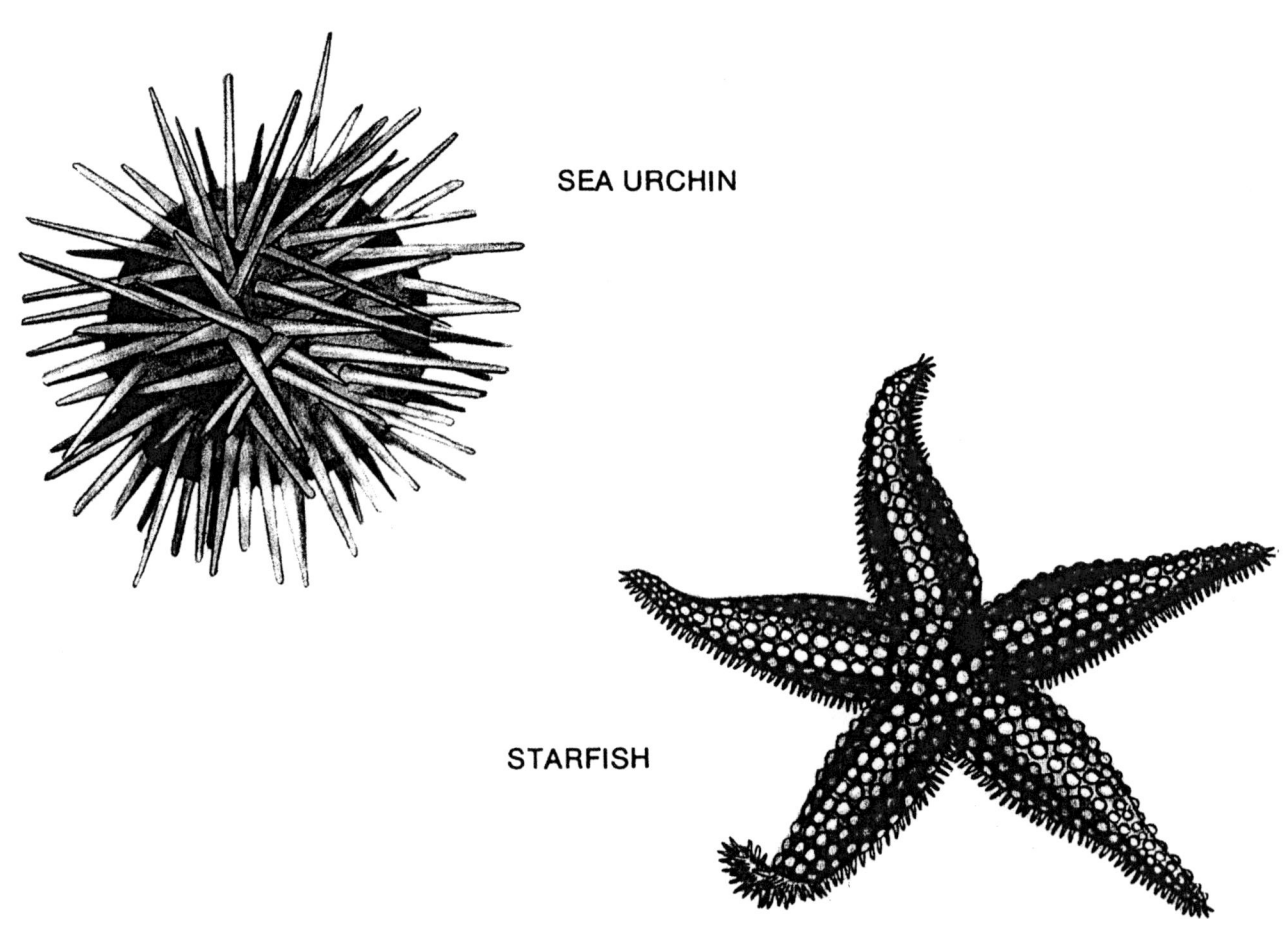

SEA URCHIN

STARFISH

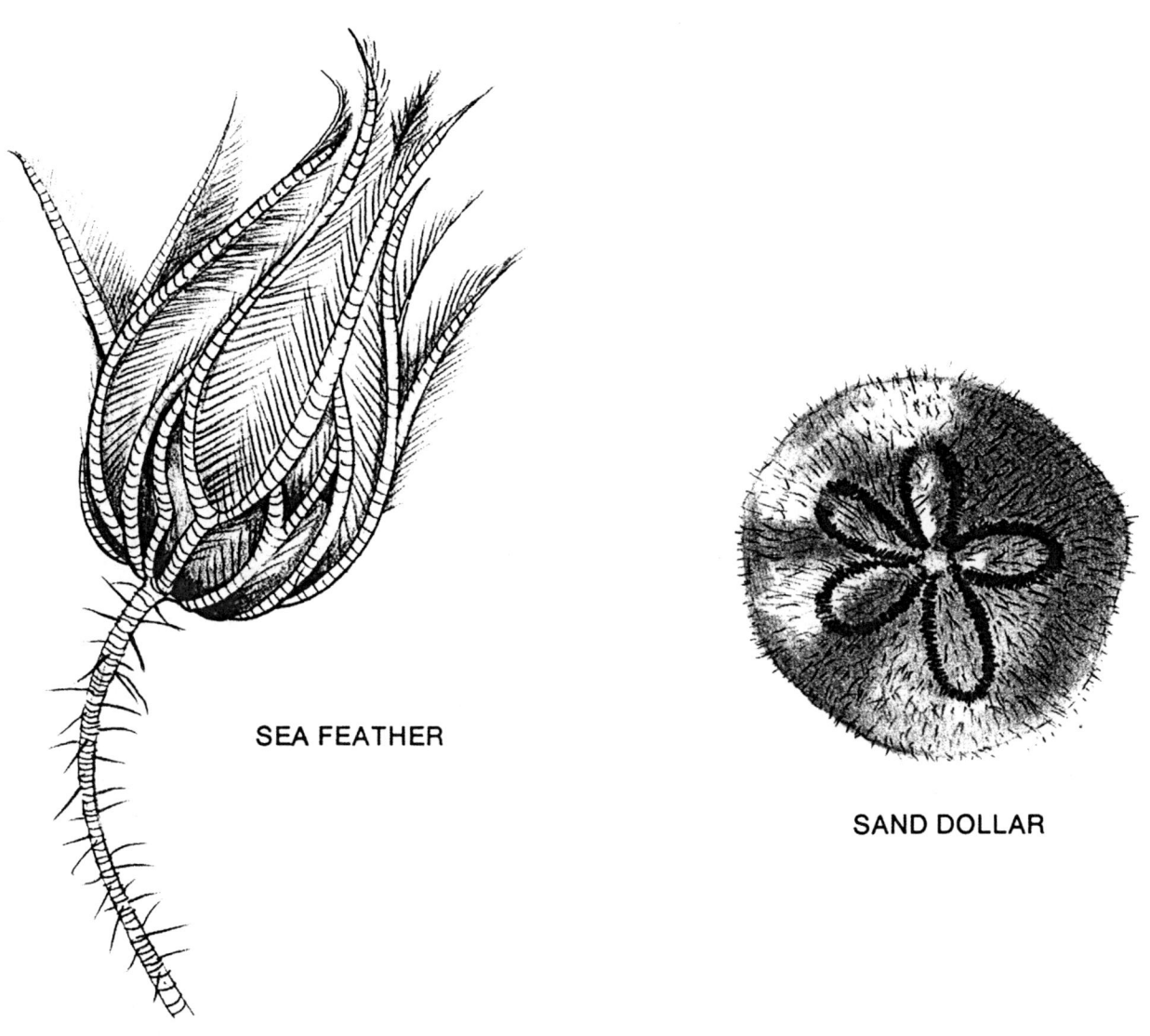

SEA FEATHER

SAND DOLLAR

Find the animal that looks like a star.
Find the animal that looks like a pincushion.
Find the animal with a flower design on the top.
Find the animal that looks as though it was
made of feathers.

51

MOLLUSKS (MOL-lusks)

These invertebrates do not have jointed legs.
They do not have a spiny skin.
But they do have a hard outside covering.
It is a shell made of lime
which covers the soft insides of the animal.

Some have two shells.

 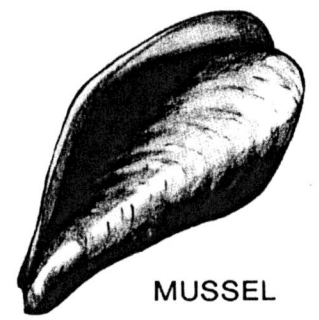 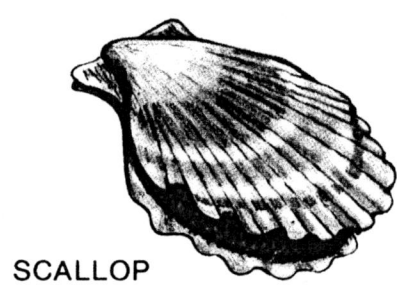

CLAM MUSSEL SCALLOP

Some have one shell.

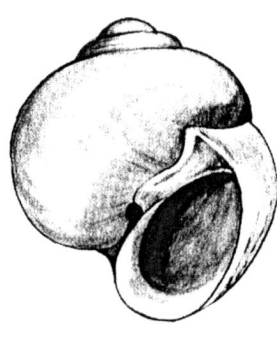 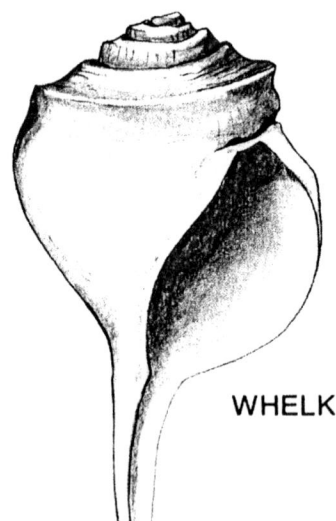 

SNAIL WHELK PERIWINKLE

Here are two exceptions to the rule. These animals
have no outside shell but their soft
insides are very much like clams, oysters,
and snails. So they are put in the same group.

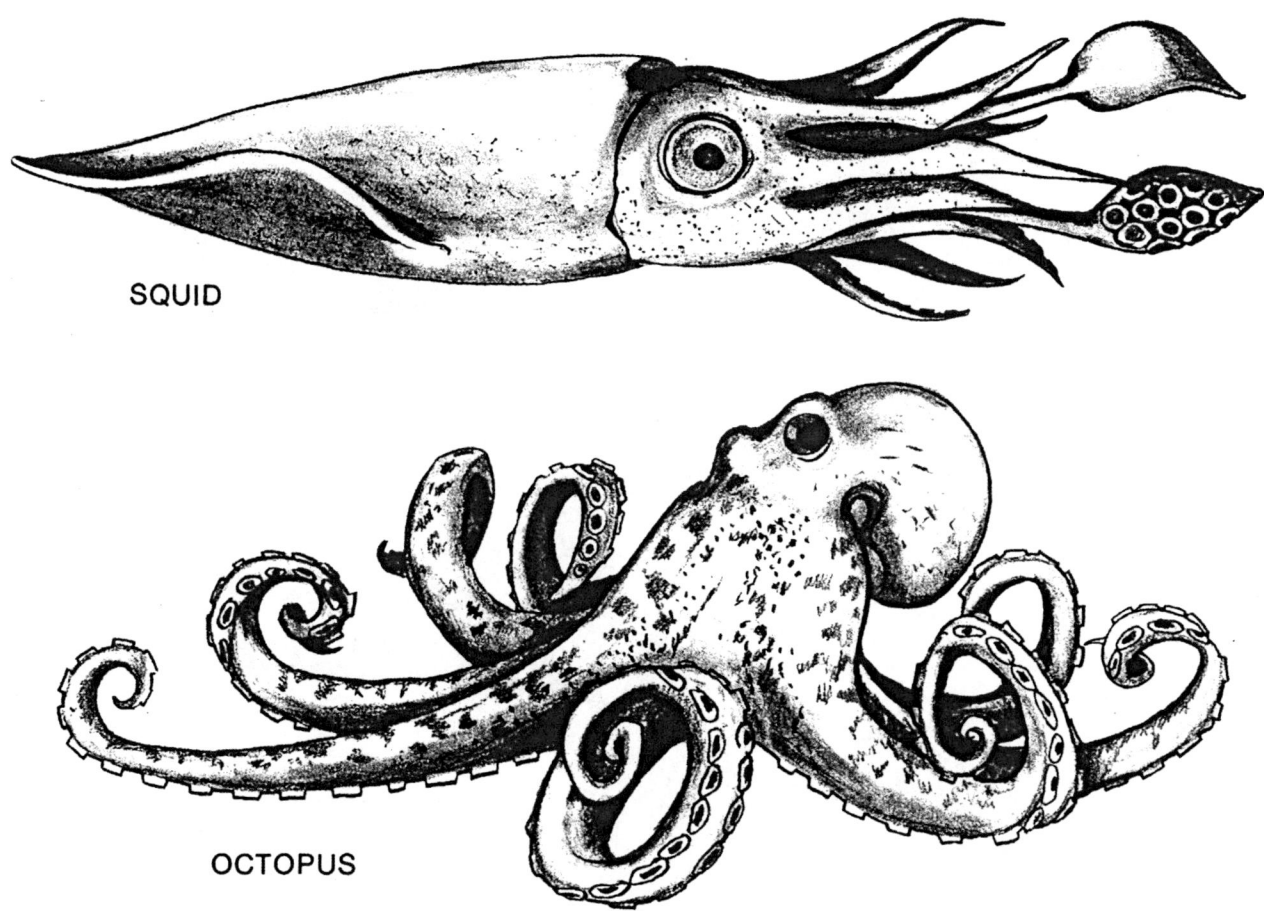

SQUID

OCTOPUS

All these invertebrates are called *mollusks.*

WORMS

Each of these worms belongs in a different group of invertebrates. Can you see any difference between them?

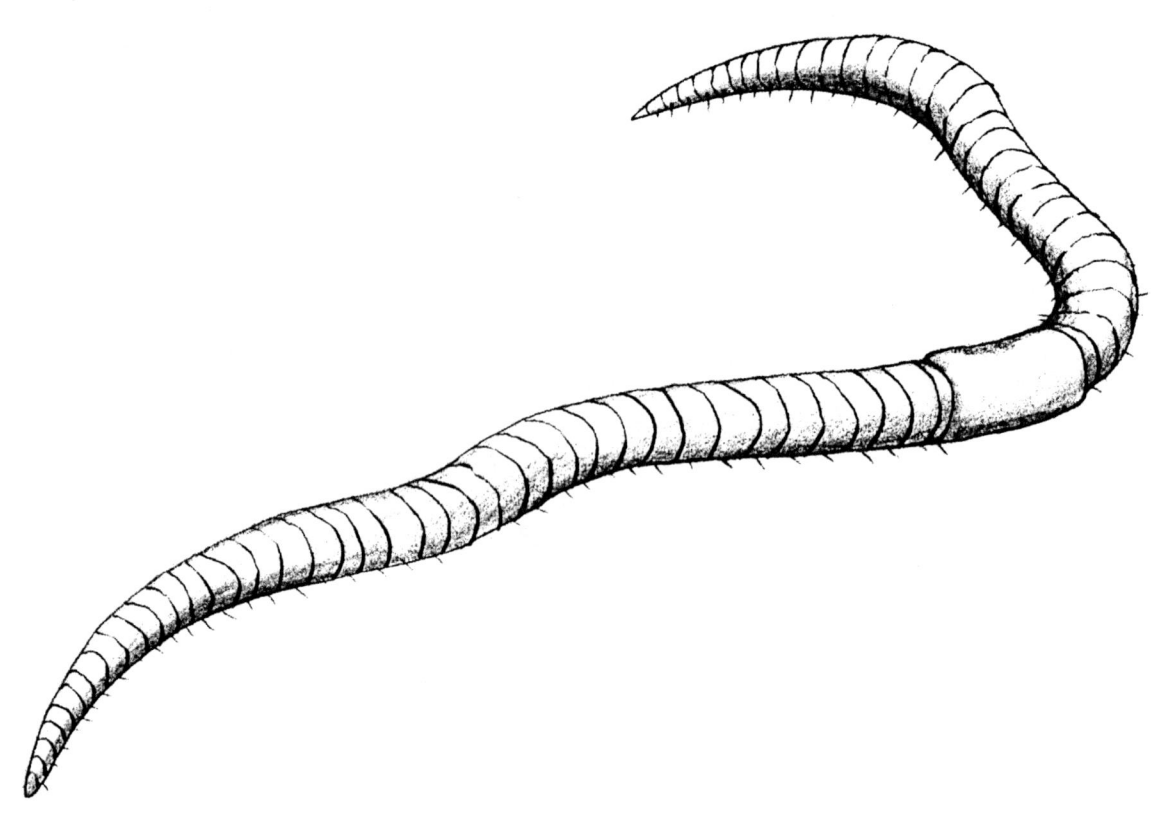

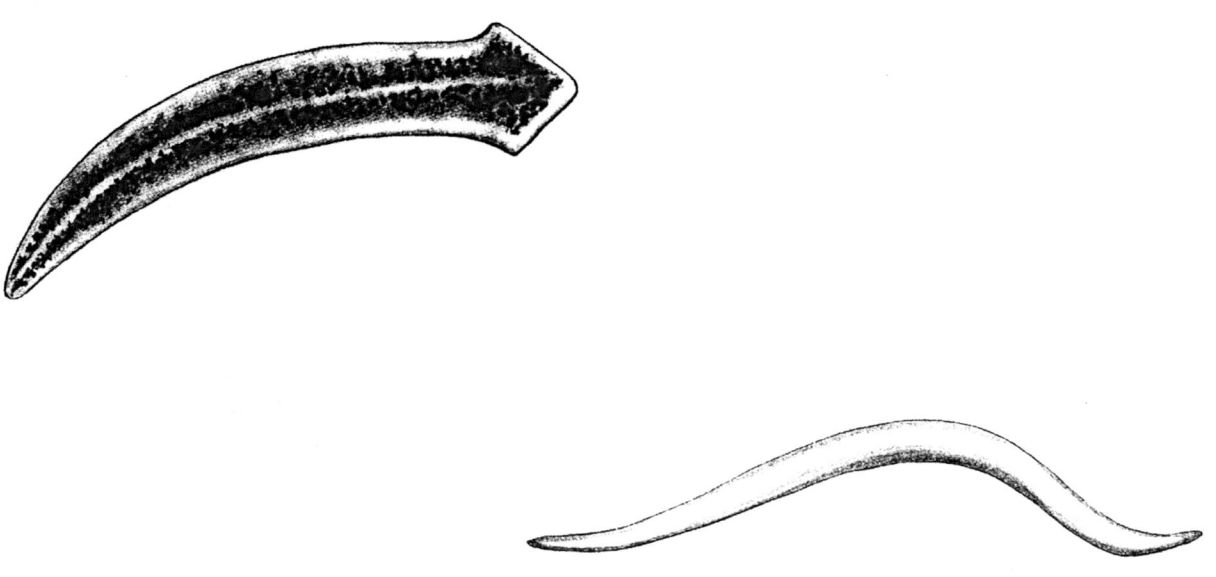

Which worm has rings around its body?
Which worm has a flat body?
Which worm is long and round like an eel?

The ringed worms are called *annelids* (AN-nel-ids).
The flat worms are called *platyhelminthes* (pla-tee-hel-MIN-theez).
The round worms are called *nemathelminthes* (ne-ma-thel-MIN-theez).

COELENTERATES (se-LEN-ter-rets)

This group of invertebrates has tentacles that can sting. Look for the tentacles on the sea anemone, jelly fish, hydra, and coral.

These invertebrates are called *coelenterates*.

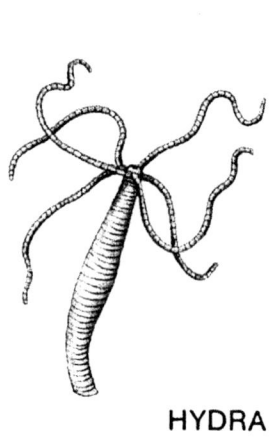

HYDRA

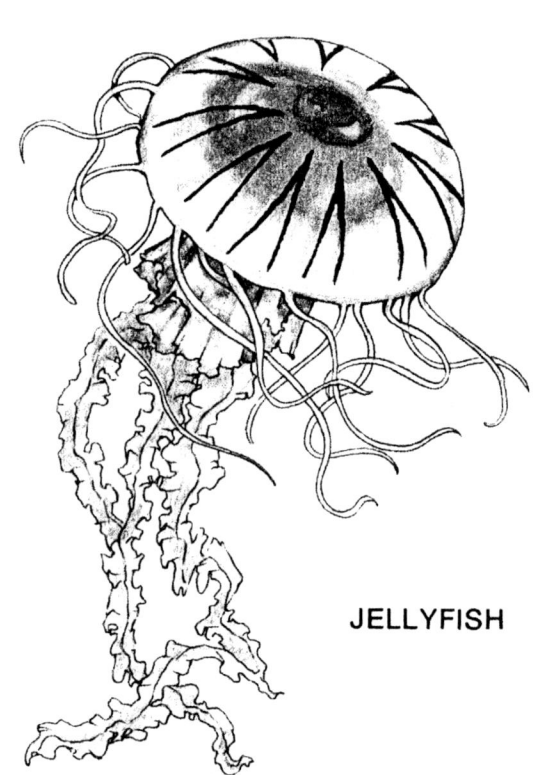

JELLYFISH

SEA ANEMONE

CORAL

Do you know two animals with tentacles
that do not sting?

Hint: See page 53.

SPONGES (SPUN-jes)

Sponges are another group of invertebrates.
The body of a sponge is a simple sac with many
holes. Water and food enter through these
holes and go out through a single large
opening.

The body wall is stiffened with a kind of
skeleton made of either glassy or chalky
needles, or spongy fibers.

The Venus Flower Basket is a glassy sponge.

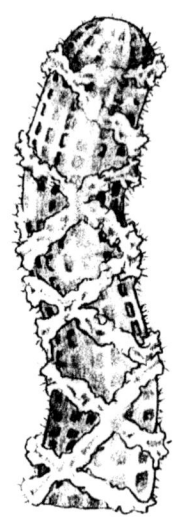

The Vase-shaped sponge is a chalky sponge.

The Elephant's Ear sponge is a spongy sponge.

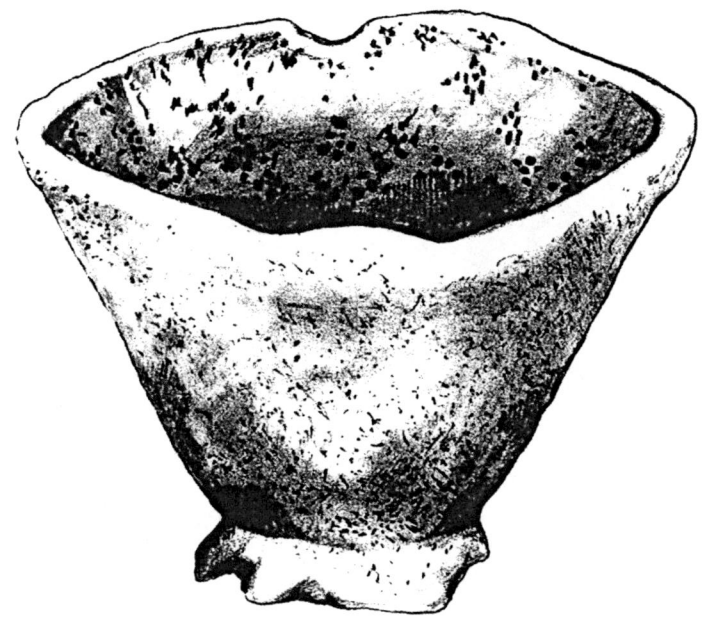

You can wash with an Elephant's Ear sponge
but the other two will scratch.

PROTOZOA (pro-ta-ZO-a)

These invertebrates called *protozoa* live in water and soil.
They are so small that most can only be seen
under a microscope.
They are one-celled animals. (A cell is the
smallest unit of life. Other animals are made
of many cells.)

There are three main kinds of protozoa
and they can be told apart by the way they move.

One kind moves little hairs (*cilia*)
like tiny oars.

One kind moves by beating a whiplike thread.

One kind moves by changing its shape.

Which is which?

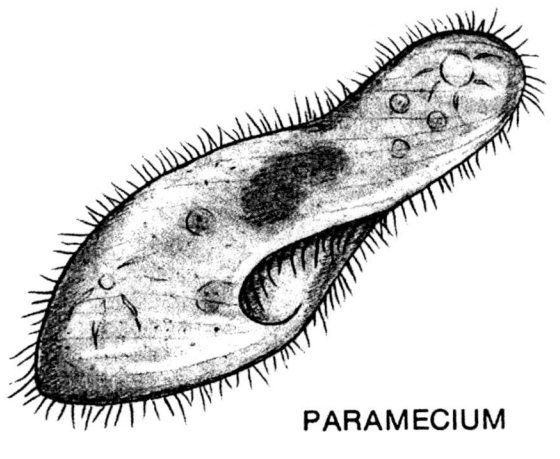

PARAMECIUM

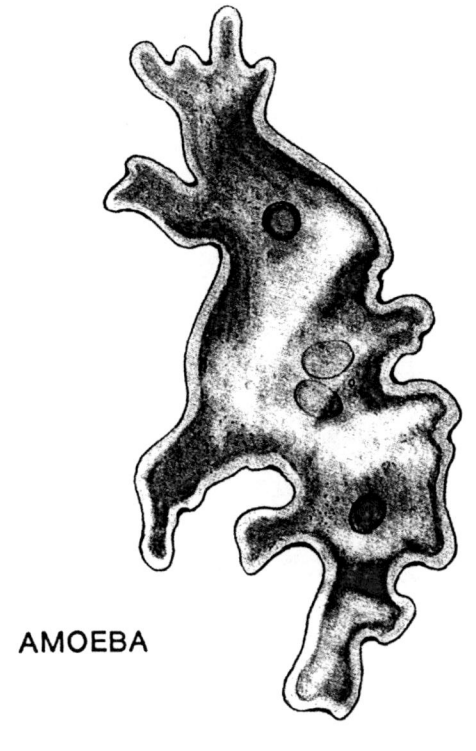

AMOEBA

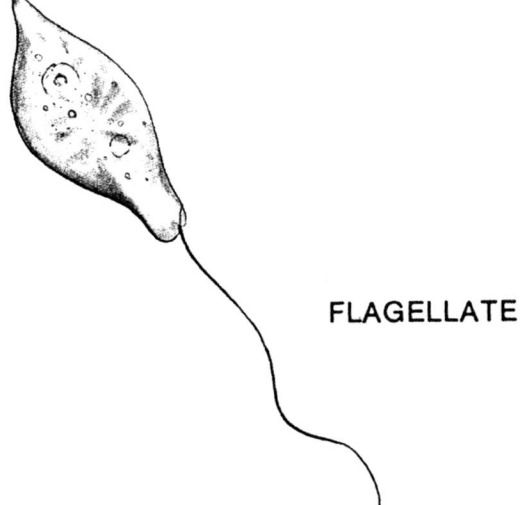

FLAGELLATE

61

INVERTEBRATES

Arthropods have jointed legs.

  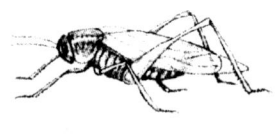

Echinoderms have spiny skins.

Mollusks have shells that cover soft bodies.

Annelids are ringed worms.

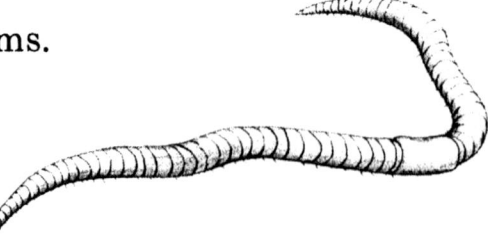

Nemathelminthes are round worms.

Platyhelminthes are flat worms.

Coelenterates have tentacles that sting.

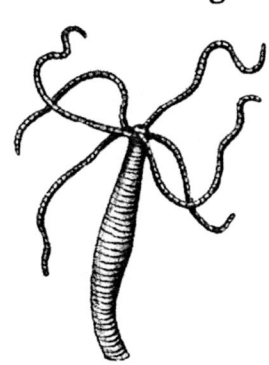

Sponges are simple sacs with pores.

Protozoa are single-celled animals.

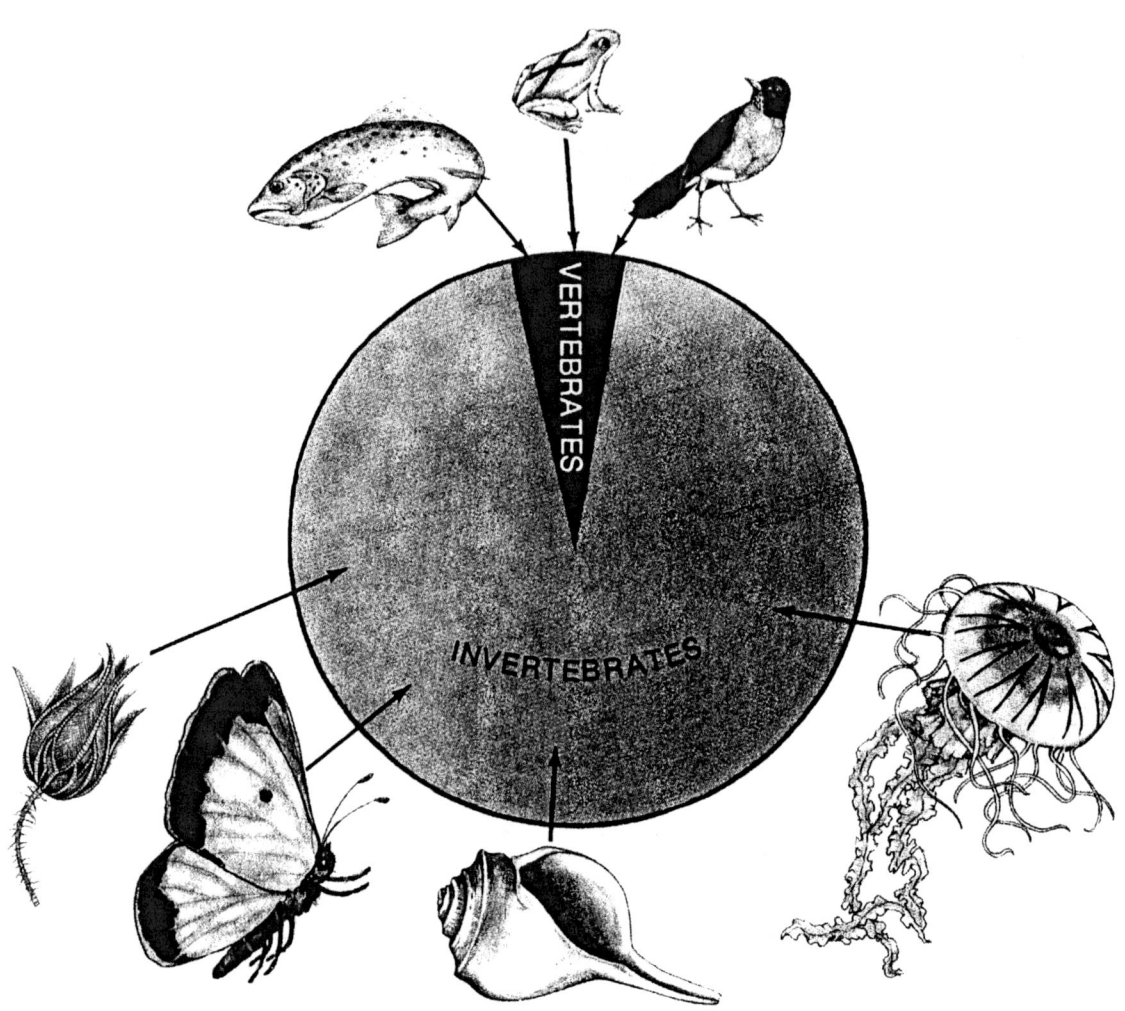

There are over one million different kinds of animals
in the world.
Only 50,000 are vertebrates.
The rest are invertebrates.

0-595-29122-8

Printed in the United States
120304LV00003BA/66/A